"Barry Rubin, a Jewish believer, has come to our rescue with this winsome, utterly lucid book — written for Gentiles who yearn to see Jewish people enter the Kingdom of God. Barry ranges widely over all the important matters—how to be credible as witnesses, how to be wise in sharing the Good News from the Hebrew Bible, how to be alert to Jewish sensibilities, how to deal honestly with Jewish barriers to faith — in short, how to be effective in bringing this restless, spiritually hungry people face to face with 'the Hope of Israel,' Jesus the Messiah."
*Arthur F. Glasser, Dean Emeritus, School of World Mission, Fuller Theological Seminary*

"It is a pleasure to commend the most enjoyable and readable book I have seen recently on sharing the Gospel with our Jewish neighbors.... I urge believers to buy this book immediately and set aside a wonderful evening of reading after they have poured a cup of coffee and set out some bagels and cream cheese. Indeed, each one who does so will be in for a wonderful treat."
*Walter C. Kaiser, Jr., Ph.D., Academic Dean, Professor of Old Testament, Trinity Evangelical Divinity School*

"God is moving among the Jewish people in an unusual way today and many of them are coming to faith. It is a unique challenge for Gentiles to share the Good News that Jesus is the Messiah with Jewish friends and neighbors. No better help is available than this book."
*Erwin J. Kolb, Th.D., Executive Director for Evangelism, the Lutheran Church — Missouri Synod*

**"You Bring the Bagels, I'll Bring the Gospel** is not only a catchy title, but a well-written, practical guide for witnessing.... Barry Rubin, a good friend and co-laborer in the field of Jewish evangelism, has done a superb job of sharing with believers the ways in which they can share their faith with Jewish people."
*Harold A. Sevener, President, Chosen People Ministries, Inc.*

# You Bring the Bagels, I'll Bring the Gospel

# You Bring the Bagels, I'll Bring the Gospel

**Barry Rubin**

Published by
chosen books

FLEMING H. REVELL COMPANY
OLD TAPPAN, NEW JERSEY

Unless noted otherwise, Scripture quotations are from the New
American Standard Bible, © The Lockman Foundation 1960, 1962,
1963, 1968, 1971, 1972, 1973, 1975, 1977.

Quotations identified JNT are taken from *Jewish New Testament* by
Dr. David Stern, © 1989 by Jewish New Testament Publications,
Jerusalem and Clarksville, Md., and used by permission.

Quotations identified KJV are taken from the King James Version of
the Bible.

Library of Congress Cataloging-in-Publication Data

Rubin, Barry, 1945–
    You bring the bagels, I'll bring the Gospel / by Barry Rubin.
      p.    cm.
    ISBN 0-8007-9149-5
    1. Jewish Christians.   2. Missions to Jews.   3. Witness bearing
(Christianity)  I. Title.
BR158.R83  1989
248'.5'088296—dc20                             89-32989
                                                CIP

Illustrations copyright © 1989 by Steffi Rubin

The Glossary of Jewish Terms, copyright © 1977 by the American
Board of Missions to the Jews, now called Chosen People Ministries, is
used by permission.

A Chosen Book
Copyright © 1989 by Barry Rubin

Chosen Books are published by
Fleming H. Revell Company
Old Tappan, New Jersey
Printed in the United States of America

# Contents

# Foreword

Many are the books and booklets telling us why and how we ought to share the life-giving message of the Gospel with our Jewish friends. Once in a while a book comes from the presses by a person who really has something meaningful to say. This latest work is by my friend Barry Rubin who, from his training as well as experience, has provided us with an excellent book.

Believers everywhere have an intellectual comprehension that the message of the New Covenant must be shared with people of all nations, including our Jewish friends. While there are excellent books on how to share God's message with people in general, God's people need to know how best to share the Gospel message of Yeshua with their Jewish friends.

Barry Rubin begins first to encourage Gentile believers to talk effectively about their faith with Jewish people. It was a Gentile believer who shared with Barry so that he became a believer. He tries to encourage the people in the churches to actually put into practice the possibility of being a good witness to a Jewish neighbor.

Barry has had excellent training in communications. He can apply those principles in such a way that the average non-Jewish believer can learn and then set out to do the job God has called us to do. Outreach to Jewish people is important.

The reader will find material on learning about the background and beliefs that might be barriers to our witness. Barry also shows us how we can overcome these barriers to have the best possible opportunity to communicate with our friends.

Of the greatest interest is Barry's analysis of how the Master Soul-winner, Yeshua, touched the hearts of people. His analysis of how Yeshua related to the Samaritan woman (John 4) is excellent and should give the average believer some expertise in how to relate to the needs of Jewish friends, and people in general.

The value of the book is enhanced by the use of numerous models that very quickly enable the Gentile believer to grasp the material and sharpen his understanding of how best to share.

Upon reading the book, I had a special blessing. You will be encouraged as you let Barry Rubin speak to your heart and allow him to guide you to be a more effective communicator as you share the Gospel with Jewish people.

Louis Goldberg, Th.D.
Professor of Theology
and Jewish Studies
Moody Bible Institute
Chicago, Illinois

# Preface

## A Message for Believers

You are about to read this book because you care about Jewish people. You have experienced new life in Jesus and you want to share this Good News with a Jewish person you know. Perhaps you have a friend, co-worker, or even a relative who is Jewish. You want to tell him or her the Gospel message—the best news you've ever heard. The news that God has provided atonement for sin. Perhaps you have known this person for years, but have not been able to discuss the Messiah. This book was written to help you share the love of Jesus with His own Jewish people.

I will be discussing the principles I have taught as both a college teacher of communications and the director of several missionary training programs. My testimony is woven throughout the book to illustrate many of the principles you will learn.

Keep in mind, however, that your responsibility is only to present the message of the Messiah as clearly as you possibly can, prayerfully and lovingly. It is not your responsibility to cause your Jewish friend to believe. That work is in the hands of God.

As you read through this book, you will see references to your "Jewish neighbor." This word *neighbor* is used in the same sense that Jesus used it in the story of the Good Samaritan. It might mean the friend next door, a distant relative, someone you work with, or anyone you encounter with a need for the Messiah. I picture your sitting down with some bagels, a cup of coffee or tea, and the Bible. What I hear is a neighborly chat about the Gospel.

From time to time I will use what is often called *Messianic* terminology—Christian concepts expressed in a Jewish way. After discussing the benefit of this terminology in your witness in Section

II, chapter 7, I use it exclusively throughout the rest of the book. This is to encourage you to become familiar with and to incorporate these Messianic terms into your own speech. It will make your message clearer.

## A Message for Jewish People

You may be wondering why a Jewish person like me would be interested in teaching non-Jewish people how to persuade you to believe in Jesus. At best, you may think that this is a waste of time. At worst, you may consider me a traitor to our people. I have one thing to say to you—truth is truth.

If Jesus—*Yeshua*, in Hebrew—is the promised Messiah, then it would make sense that Jews should believe in what He says. If He is not, then not only am I wasting time, but it would follow that all Christians are practicing a false religion and should look elsewhere for truth. Yeshua claimed to be our long-awaited Messiah. Either He is or He isn't.

In this book, although it is written to help non-Jewish followers of His communicate His message more effectively to you, you may discover that Yeshua really is who He said He is—the Messiah. Why not prayerfully ask God to show you the truth?

Once, an agnostic friend and I were having a discussion. It took awhile, but he finally admitted that God's existence had nothing whatsoever to do with his faith or lack of it. Either God exists or He doesn't. My friend's belief or disbelief had no effect upon the reality of God. Logic tells us that God exists (or doesn't exist) regardless of what we believe.

So it is with the question of Yeshua. Either He is the Promised One, the Messiah of Israel and Savior of the world, or He is not. Both statements cannot be true. Our belief does not make Him the Messiah (*Christ*, in Greek); our unbelief does not turn Him into fiction.

I believe that Yeshua is exactly who He said He was—the Messiah. I came to this conclusion in 1973 and the longer I study and ponder His claim, the more convinced I am of its truth.

To Jewish people who read this book, I ask you to try to

understand that Christians who purchase this book do so out of sincere love. They want to administer the antidote for man's greatest ailment—sin. The cure is found in Yeshua.

We who have come into a personal relationship with the God of Abraham, Isaac, and Jacob through Yeshua, the Messiah, know that He really is "the way, the truth, and the life." Pray that God would give you an open mind as you look at this book. Don't be afraid to consider the Messiahship of Yeshua.

## People I Thank for Making This Book Possible

My professors of communication at Ohio University, who taught me about interpersonal communication.

Dr. Henry and Marie Einspruch, founders of The Lederer Foundation in Baltimore, Maryland, who provided literature that had a major impact on my life. Dan and Arlene Rigney, whose love and patience enabled me to see the truth that the Messiah had come. Moishe Rosen, who taught me much about communicating the Good News to our people, the Jewish people. Pat Klein who gave me encouragement as I wrote this book. Dr. Louis Goldberg, who has been a friend for many years and willingly read over and commented on my manuscript.

My wife, Steffi, who not only gave her illustrations, capturing the content of each chapter of the book, but also shared my ideas with me and helped me find more effective ways of saying them. Rebecca and Shira, my lovely daughters, who gave me the time and space to write. My parents, who brought me up with an appreciation for my Jewish heritage and an identification with my people.

And, of course, I thank God and His Messiah, through whom I have been given eternal and abundant life.

# INTRODUCTION

## Catching Fish for the Messiah
### —or—
### *It's the Perfect Time to Drop Your Line!*

When I was a young boy, I saw a cartoon (Disney, I think) that "taught" how to fish. One scene greatly impressed me. Each time the fisherman tossed in his line he landed a big one. Soon he had a pile of fish on the shore as tall as he. *Wow, that looks like fun,* I thought. Since there was a small lake in my little Maryland town, I decided to try my hand at fishing. It looked so easy.

Grabbing a broom handle and tying a string to the end of it, I marched with determination down to the lake and dropped in my line. After what seemed like days—probably an hour or two—I headed home discouraged, dejected, and definitely finished with fishing . . . forever! I hadn't even gotten one nibble.

That evening my dad came home from work and found me sitting on the porch, head in hands.

"What's wrong?" he asked, reading my sad expression. I told him about my totally unproductive fishing expedition. Trying not to look too amused, my father questioned me about my fishing techniques.

"What did you use for bait?"

"Bait?" I repeated. "What's bait?"

"It's what you put on the end of the hook."

"Oh," I said. "What's a hook?"

Apparently I had missed some of the fundamentals of fishing. All I had seen was that cartoon character catching fish. Apparently I had missed what he had done to prepare to catch those fish. Dad explained about hooks and bait. Was I relieved to know that I didn't have to give up fishing forever!

Sometimes, listening to believers discuss their witness to Jewish people reminds me of that first fishing trip. In their zeal to "catch a fish" they overlook the fundamentals. They give it a try but come home discouraged, dejected, definitely finished with "fishing." I don't want that to happen to you. I want you to be effective in your witnessing so that you don't become discouraged. After all, how are my fellow Jewish people going to hear the Gospel if Gentile believers are too discouraged to share it with them?

Jesus promised that He would make His disciples "fishers of men." There are fundamentals of this fishing that you need to learn in order to share the Gospel effectively with Jewish people. That's the purpose of this book.

To help organize all the material you will be learning, I've included for you what I call a witnessing model. It's something I used when I taught college communications and then applied to the training programs I've conducted that teach Jewish evangelism.

## WITNESSING MODEL
## FOR JEWISH EVANGELISM

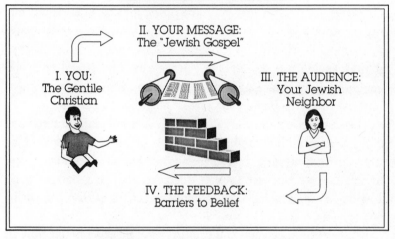

The book is divided into four sections:
   I) You: The Gentile Christian
   II) Your Message: The "Jewish Gospel"
   III) The Audience: Your Jewish Neighbor
   IV) The Feedback: Barriers to Belief

Section I is about you, the Gentile Christian. I know that in the Messiah Jews and Gentiles are one and that the "middle wall of partition" has been broken down. Yet, there are still individual distinctives that remain. Sharing the Gospel with Jewish people is a form of cross-cultural communication. Therefore, you'll need to learn how the differences between Jews and Gentiles can be used to help get the message of the Messiah across. This section will help you understand your role in Jewish evangelism.

I speak in Section II of the "Jewish Gospel." While it's true that there is only one Gospel of salvation for Jews and Gentiles, there are many ways to present it. Those involved with child evangelism have learned special ways to communicate the Gospel to little ones. Those working with college students have developed outreach approaches that are effective on campuses. This same principle holds true for Jewish people. Section II will teach you how to share the Good News in a "Jewish" way.

Section III will help you better understand your Jewish neighbor. It would be foolish to imply that after reading a few pages in this book, you will really *know* your Jewish neighbor. That would not only be impossible, it would be presumptuous. Getting to know someone takes time. Nevertheless, a look into Jewish history, religion, and culture should offer you a greater understanding of the people to whom your neighbor belongs. You yourself would know best how to get to know your Jewish neighbor as a friend.

The last section, Section IV, will discuss the unique responses your Jewish neighbor might offer as you present the Gospel. Not only will we deal with the more common Jewish objections to the Gospel, but we will also look at questions that may not really be questions and talk about how to apply principles of discernment in your witness.

Let me encourage you. You couldn't have picked a better time to get involved in Jewish evangelism. Not since the first century have so many Jewish people come to believe in Jesus.

No one can give exact numbers, but I have heard estimates that there are more than 100,000 Jewish believers in the United States and 350,000 worldwide. A Jewish believer from London told me recently that he thinks there are 5,000 Jewish believers in that city alone.

One very visible evidence of the existence of these large numbers of Jewish believers is the rise in what has become known as the Messianic congregational movement. Whereas twenty years ago you might have found small pockets of Jewish believers meeting for weekly Bible study, today you can visit any of the hundreds of congregations where Jewish and Gentile believers in Jesus worship

God in a distinctively Jewish style. There are Messianic congregations and fellowships all over the world. Summer conferences that attract thousands interested in the Jewish expression of faith in Jesus lend further credence to the claim that this is the day for Jewish evangelism. And the movement is growing!

The impact of God's Spirit moving among Jewish people is also underlined by the recent appearance of several groups who counter the witness of those they call "tricky missionaries." Misunderstanding the loving purpose of those who spread the Gospel, these groups suspect the motives of missionaries and warn the Jewish people away from their message. We know that God is at work because the opposition is busy as well.

Now, understanding the structure of this book and believing that you *can* be a successful fisherman for the Messiah, let's begin by taking a look at you, the Gentile Christian.

# SECTION I

# You: The Gentile Christian

As you can see from our witnessing model, *you* begin the process. Some have concluded that reaching Jewish people is a job solely for the professional missionary. I do not think so. I am convinced that Gentiles have a specific job to do in Jewish evangelism. Apparently you agree, or you would not be reading this book.

Section I is all about you and how you fit into the plan for Israel's salvation. Chapter 1 discusses what God has said about the need to witness to His chosen people. It can help you appreciate the biblical basis for Jewish evangelism and how it fits into the plans and purposes of God.

In case you start to think, "Who, me? A Gentile, witness to a Jew?" I've included chapter 2 to encourage you. You'll not only see why Gentiles are often more effective witnessing to Jews, but you'll also see how God planned for you, a non-Jew, to be a part of the process of reaching Jewish people for Jesus, the Messiah.

Everyone who witnesses does so within a context. I've already shared with you how this is a very encouraging time to be talking to Jews about Jesus. But realize, too, that this comes at the end of a 2,000-year drought. Chapter 3 will review certain events of history that pertain to the "Church"* and her relationship to the Jewish people. Some of the story is not pretty. It's not written to instill guilt, but to help make you aware of all possible reasons Jewish people may hesitate to learn about Jesus.

The last chapter of Section I offers some suggestions for becoming more credible in your testimony. We know it is the Word of God, covered with much prayer, that wins souls. There is truth, however, in the notion that the message is inextricably linked to its messenger. As you will see, the apostle Paul spoke about this very issue of credibility.

So let's now turn the spotlight on you, a Gentile believer in Jesus, with a heartfelt desire to share the love of the Messiah with your Jewish neighbor. There are those people and forces who will attempt to discourage you from your pursuit. The following chapter should help you stand firm in your conviction to witness to the lost sheep of the house of Israel.

---

*From time to time through the text, you will notice that the words *Church* or *Christian* appear in quotation marks. This is to emphasize that there have been individuals who, though calling themselves Christians or identifying with the Church, have not always behaved like true followers of Jesus. This is particularly noteworthy when it comes to certain historical events concerning the Jewish people. It is difficult to believe that those who persecuted Jesus' people could truly be classified as His disciples. Throughout the book, when referring to true followers of Jesus, I most often use the term *believer*.

# 1

# Should Jews Really Be Persuaded to Believe in Jesus?

## —or—

## *Should I Just Leave My Neighbor Alone?*

Something seems to be happening in several of the mainline denominations. Theologians call it *liberalism*, getting away from the plain and simple Gospel message that Jesus died to pay the debt for our sins and that by accepting His atoning work on our behalf we are granted eternal life.

Concurrent with this liberal position, we find many leaders steering their denominations and churches away from evangelizing Jewish people. They probably mean well, attempting to be sensitive to those who have suffered centuries of untold prejudice and persecution in the name of Christ. But they unknowingly do Jewish people terrible harm by withholding from them the Good News of the Messiah, Jesus. By neglecting to present the message of salvation to the people for whom it was first intended, they unwittingly commit the ultimate act of anti-Semitism: They withhold the message of salvation from the Jews.

I know you don't agree with these church leaders. You picked up this book to learn more about sharing the Messiah with His people. But, because of the commitment of some *not* to share the Messiah with Jews, it is all the more important to know why you should. In addition to the fact that Jesus died to atone for everyone's sins, Jews' as well as Gentiles', there are four special reasons to share the Messiah with Jewish people.

## It Identifies Us with Our Spiritual Heroes

Growing up in Maryland, I looked forward to that first chill of autumn. It meant just one thing: football season! And, like other young boys, I had a hero. His name was Johnny Unitas, quarterback for the then-Baltimore, now-Indianapolis Colts. "Johnny U," we called him. He was perhaps the finest quarterback ever to play the game. Since I, too, played that position, it was natural for me to identify strongly with him. I wore his number, number 19. I tried to throw the ball the way he did. I even got a flat-top haircut to look

like him. In every way I could, I attempted to d
of my hero's life.

Then, when winter thawed into spring, foo
memory and baseball preoccupied my young
Mantle stood tall upon my hero's pedestal. Having sp.
formative month of life in the Bronx, I naturally pledged my
allegiance to the New York Yankees, the "Bronx Bombers." And
back in the '50s, "the Mick" was the man to emulate. Whatever
"the Mick" was, that was what I longed to be.

Modeling ourselves after successful people, imitating those
whom we desire to be like, is a way to grow into that image. Why
do business people who want to get ahead read magazines like *Money*
or *Fortune*? On those pages they find role models.

What individual interested in becoming physically fit wants to
exercise with an aerobics teacher who is fat and lumpy? No, we all
search for models to identify with, to copy. Their success encourages
us to strive to reach our own goals.

As we look through the Scriptures, we find something interesting
about role models. The spiritual goals of those people we admire
often relate to their spiritual nurture of the Jewish people. Many of
our biblical heroes had great concern for their Jewish brothers and
sisters.

Moses is a spiritual role model for many. He strove to complete
his ultimate goal of leading the children of Israel home. True, he fell
short, but it wasn't for lack of concern and dedication.

Once, after the Israelites built a golden calf, directly disobeying
the first of the Ten Commandments, Moses interceded:

"But now, if Thou wilt, forgive their sin—and if not, please blot
me out from Thy book which Thou hast written!"

EXODUS 32:32

Moses was willing to give up his life for this wayward, rebellious
people.

The apostle Paul is also a well-known role model who worked to
spread the Good News far and wide. While he is revered as the
Jewish apostle to the Gentiles, like Moses he, too, had deep concern

wn people. In the midst of his doctrinal letter to the largely
le church at Rome, Paul was inspired to insert his feelings on
s subject:

> I have great sorrow and unceasing grief in my heart. For I could
> wish that I myself were accursed, *separated* from Christ [Messiah]
> for the sake of my brethren, my kinsmen according to the flesh,
> who are Israelites.
>
> ROMANS 9:2–4

As believers in Jesus, we choose Him as our ultimate role model.
Our goal is to grow spiritually. To be Messiah-like. To be like
Jesus. Paul thought that believers ought "to become conformed to
the image of His [God's] Son" (Romans 8:29). An important part of
that goal of becoming like Jesus is recognizing His deep concern for
His people, the Jews. Weeping over Jerusalem, Jesus cried,

> "O Jerusalem, Jerusalem, who kills the prophets and stones those
> who are sent to her! How often I wanted to gather your children
> together, the way a hen gathers her chicks under her wings, and
> you were unwilling."
>
> MATTHEW 23:37

This is only one of the many verses that reveal the Messiah's heart
for His people. Even while dying on the cross, He extended His
compassion to His confused, misdirected brethren and the Romans
who actually crucified Him, saying, "Father forgive them; for they
do not know what they are doing" (Luke 23:34).

Thus, we see from these examples that Moses, Paul, and, of
course, Messiah Jesus, had a common burden for the salvation of the
Jewish people. Each was willing to sacrifice himself for the
accomplishment of that goal. If we are to grow into the likeness of
the Messiah and become more like heroes of Scripture, we, too,
must assume that burden and give of ourselves that many of the
nation of Israel might receive God's forgiveness and love.

## It's a Good Investment

A second reason for sharing the Gospel with Jewish people is that
you will receive a very good return on your investment of time and

love. And that is due to the zeal of the Jewish people. Former *New York Times* reporter McCandlish Phillips, in his book *The Bible, The Supernatural, and the Jews* (Bethany Fellowship, Minneapolis, 1970), wrote a chapter entitled "The Influence of the Jews," in which he states:

> Jews are socially and culturally influential. They cannot avoid being influential as a people. In any society in which they are found, Jews are influential out of proportion to their numbers. They affect the history of the nation they are in and they affect its culture. To a significant extent the history and culture of the nation will turn on what some Jews do. It is written into the very nature of the Jews, by the finger of God, to be influential (p. 279).

Consider the enormous impact individual Jews have had on history. For a people of such small numbers, the impact is disproportionate. Phillips reminds us of "Moses . . . Jesus . . . Marx . . . Freud . . . Einstein [and he says that] such Jews have had a vast impact and influence on the affairs of mankind." According to M. Hirsch Goldberg, in his entertaining as well as enlightening book *The Jewish Connection* (Stein & Day, New York, 1976),

> Mark Twain, surveying the wide-ranging activity of Jews in his day, once cracked that there must be at least 25 million Jews living in America. Of course, at no time during Twain's life were there more than 2 million Jews in the country. Twain, generally friendly to Jews, was simply expressing a feeling shared by friend and foe alike—Jews just seem to be all over (p. 107).

Twain also pointed out that the mere existence of the Jews as an intact people is convincing proof of the existence of God!

Have things changed much since Twain penned his remarks? Not really. Jews still influence the world around them. Henry Kissinger. Leonard Bernstein. Dr. Joyce Brothers. George Burns. Howard Cosell. (I didn't say were always loved, just influential!) Paul Newman. And on and on.

This phenomenon is something that the apostle Paul described in Romans 10:1–2:

> Brethren, my heart's desire and my prayer to God for them is for their salvation. For I bear them witness that they have a zeal for God, but not in accordance with knowledge.

This zeal, which often manifests itself in influence, was originally planted within the Jewish people by God and intended to serve His purpose. God planned to bless the entire world through His people. That's why He said to Abram, "And in you all the families of the earth shall be blessed" (Genesis 12:3).

It was a blessing to the world that two Jews, Salk and Sabin, conquered polio. It has been a blessing to enjoy the comedic and dramatic talents of Milton Berle, Jack Benny, Jerry Lewis, and Dustin Hoffman. And who wouldn't agree, after a hard day's work, that it's a blessing to come home and slip into your most comfortable pair of Levis (as in Levi Strauss) or Calvins (as in Calvin Klein)?

Think of all the constructive, helpful, and charitable contributions that Jews have provided—from medicine to music, movies to science, literature and art to scholarship. Imagine what a blessing it will be to the Kingdom of God when this talent becomes devoted directly to God and His Messiah!

It was for the purpose of blessing that God granted the Jewish people another unique ability: "You shall remember the Lord your God, for it is He who is giving you power to make wealth" (Deuteronomy 8:18). Some have become resentful, generalizing that Jewish people do well in business. But they forget that, as a result of this often-true fact, Jews also contribute enormous amounts to charities and in taxes.

God-given talent combined with God-given zeal has indeed worked together for the good of all mankind.

The Jews of Jesus' day, much like Orthodox Jews today, had a tremendous zeal for God; but their zeal was not according to complete biblical revelation. Most Jewish people, then as now, have unfortunately missed the Messiah. Paul wrote:

For not knowing about God's righteousness, and seeking to establish their own, they did not subject themselves to the righteousness of God. For Christ [Messiah] is the end of the law for righteousness to everyone who believes.

ROMANS 10:3–4

This attempt to attain righteousness through good works can be seen more clearly on Jewish high holy days than at other times of the year. Jewish people flock to synagogues hoping, through their attendance and recited prayers, to achieve atonement for their sins. This is without the benefit of the Temple or sacrificial system. In so many tragic ways it is an empty gesture, designed to clear the conscience, not cleanse the soul. God spoke through Moses:

> "For the life of the flesh is in the blood, and I have given it to you on the altar to make atonement for your souls."
>
> LEVITICUS 17:11

Only through the sacrifice of Jesus can true reconciliation with God be attained. The intense religiosity of the holiday season is what might be called "misdirected zeal." When zeal is directed toward God, blessings for the Kingdom result. Focused on the needs of the world, this fervor brings blessings to the world. But when this God-given passion is turned against God, it causes problems. Karl Marx, the founder of Communism, was an atheistic Jew.

This zeal manifests itself in fields that have nothing much to do with tradition or truth. The enthusiasm that was designed and built into the Jews by God often finds expression in some very non-Jewish and not particularly biblical activities. My own "misdirected zeal" led me down a confusing and dangerous path until God set my feet on solid ground.

Since I was not a very religious Jew, I was not particularly concerned with keeping the laws and traditions of my people; I leveled my sights toward the lofty pursuit of Truth. I spent my young adult life engrossed in psychology books, philosophy books, and the study of the religions of the world. Finally I became initiated into the newly packaged ancient art of transcendental meditation, or T.M., a disguised form of Hinduism.

T.M. is a movement popularized by the Maharishi Mahesh Yogi, a man who gained renown when the Beatles subscribed to his teachings. Purporting to be a technique for relaxation, T.M. promises to enable people to achieve their highest human potential. From where I sat, it sounded intriguing.

It was the late 1960s. Tensions within the United States ran high. Blacks and whites struggled with the question of racial equality. Students actively protested a war that raged in Vietnam. Drugs and divorce were becoming epidemic.

Living in Washington, D.C., a white teaching at a black university, I felt a unique kind of tension all around me. A "simple technique to relieve stress and strain" sounded like just what the doctor ordered.

Furthermore, the prospect of achieving my full human potential also appealed to me. It had become a personal goal, something I believed everyone should strive for.

So with customary Jewish zeal, I dove into the practice of transcendental meditation, becoming convinced early on that the salvation of the world depended upon everyone's meditating according to the tenets of T.M. So convinced was I that I enrolled in a teacher training program.

I discovered that the second-in-command to the Maharishi was a Jewish man. I, along with thousands of other Jewish people, found myself heading intently toward a religion terribly foreign and diametrically opposed to the faith of our fathers.

I should have noticed what I was getting into from the beginning. The initiation ceremony included presenting an offering of fruit, flowers, and incense to the gods of Hinduism. Oh, there was also the offering of $75, the price of finding "god" at that time. (Inflation has driven the price substantially higher now.)

I should have become wary when, in the teacher-training program, the Maharishi expounded the Hindu scriptures. I should have noticed that my supposed "unique" *mantra* (the sound I repeated over and over to help me meditate) was the same sound received by many others. My eyes should have opened when I heard reports of meditators having mental breakdowns during long meditation courses. And when I began to get more and more self- rather than other-oriented, I should have recognized that T.M. was antithetical to the Bible's message of love. But, as I will explain later, it wasn't until God Himself broke through that I discovered my misdirected zeal was dangerous for me and others.

The apostle Paul, discussing the phenomenon of Jewish unbelief, said,

> If their transgression be riches for the world and their failure be riches for the Gentiles, how much more will their fulfillment be!
>
> ROMANS 11:12

What I think he meant is just what we've been discussing here. Redirecting this God-given zeal, focusing it toward the work of God—especially the proclamation of the Gospel—is a potentially powerful tool for blessing! This, after all, was the task for which the Jews were originally created and to which we were called. And according to Revelation 7:4, it's exactly what 144,000 Jewish people will be busy doing sometime in the not-too-distant future!

God gave the Jews zeal, a supernaturally bestowed drive and enthusiasm, for the purpose of blessing the entire world. It would certainly seem that in many aspects of our lives, Jewish people have indeed been a blessing. But how much greater the blessing will be when this zeal, this drive, this intensity is directed toward the purposes for which God initially intended it—to bring light to the nations, to declare the testimony of a faithful living God, to share with the world the love of His Messiah.

Reaching out to Jewish people can be a great investment of your time, money, and energies. Think of how having a hand in redirecting that Jewish zeal can change the world for God. It's simply good stewardship.

## It Will Get Results

A theme runs through the Scripture that is often untaught—the theme of the *remnant*. This concept helps explain the fact that while some people seek God and follow His teachings, others do not. Because this remnant exists today among the Jews, we have God's guarantee that our witnessing will produce results.

You could say that the remnant began back in the Garden of Eden. Abel was part of the remnant; Cain was not. Later, Isaac was part of the remnant; Ishmael was not. Jacob was; Esau was not.

In Romans 11, Paul introduced this concept of the remnant in his argument for Jewish evangelism. He asked rhetorically, "God has not rejected His people, has He?" His impassioned response was, "May it never be!" Paul considered himself part of the remnant of Jewish people who believed. He referred to 7,000 faithful believers in the days of Elijah "who [had] not bowed the knee to Baal." He went on to say, "In the same way then, there has also come to be at the present time a remnant according to God's gracious choice." (See Romans 11:1–5.)

There *still* is a remnant.

Not since the first century have so many Jews come to believe that Jesus is the promised Messiah. In addition to the hundreds of Messianic congregations in this country that I have already mentioned, there are also thousands of Jewish people who attend traditional churches. Perhaps this number may not seem to be a large percentage of the total current U.S. Jewish population of about six million. But a remnant is just that—a remnant.

Just a few years ago those who worked in the field of Jewish evangelism often harvested little fruit. Undaunted by the slow response, they believed what they could not see—that there was, according to God's Word, a remnant waiting to respond. Today, perhaps because of their faithfulness, the work of witnessing to Jewish people is being blessed with abundant reward. Seed sown in the past is producing ripe fruit and much of it is ready for picking.

There are, for instance, times when I have shared the message of the Messiah with Jewish people and received immediate results. Recently it was with a 76-year-old Jewish lady who just needed a little nudge in order to profess her faith. Another time it was with a young man who came to our congregation. Like the Philippian jailer in Acts 16, his question was, "What must I do to be saved?"

This means it is entirely possible that *your* neighbor, co-worker, or friend might be part of the remnant, waiting to respond to the Good News. If you learn to communicate the message of the Messiah effectively you will be giving that friend an opportunity to receive God's blessing.

## It Will Reap a Reward from God

I don't know why He does it, but the Bible makes it clear that God blesses those who bless the Jews. Going back to Genesis, we find that this unusual promise was first given to Abram, the father of the Jewish people: "And I will bless those who bless you, and the one who curses you I will curse" (Genesis 12:3). History, seen in the following examples from Scripture, has proved the truth of this unique promise.

Abraham's son Isaac settled in Gerar, land of Abimelech, king of the Philistines. There was no love lost between Abimelech's people and the family of Abraham, but when Abimelech saw how God made Isaac prosper, in spite of the Philistines' displeasure toward him, Abimelech went to Isaac and said:

> "We see plainly that the Lord has been with you; so we said, 'Let there now be an oath between us . . . that you will do us no harm, just as we have not touched you and have done to you nothing but good, and have sent you away in peace. You are now the blessed of the Lord.' "
>
> GENESIS 26:28–29

Bad blood or no, Abimelech did not want to be on the wrong side of God.

As he was dying, Isaac repeated God's promise to his son Jacob: "Cursed be those who curse you, and blessed be those who bless you" (Genesis 27:29). Even though Isaac did not know which son he was blessing, it is crystal clear that he wanted to reiterate God's promise that it is better to bless the Jewish people than to curse them.

Consistent as the Lord is, this warning held true throughout the Old Testament. The Egyptian Pharaoh who held the Israelites in slavery was a classic case of someone who "passed over" being blessed and got cursed instead. He would not allow the Israelites to take a three-day journey into the wilderness to worship God, and what did he get? A bloody Nile, frogs galore, lice, insects, diseased livestock, boils, hail, locusts, darkness, the death of all the firstborn of Egypt, and, finally, the exodus of the Israelites from Egypt at the expense of his own army (Exodus 5–14). It would have been better for him to have gotten God's message about blessing the Jews in the first place.

Rahab the harlot was a lot smarter than Pharaoh when it came to blessing and cursing. She told the Israelites who had come to spy on her city of Jericho,

> "I know that the Lord has given you the land. . . . For we have heard how the Lord dried up the water of the Red Sea before you . . . for the Lord your God, He is God in heaven above and on earth beneath. Now therefore, please swear to me by the Lord, since I have dealt kindly with you, that you also will deal kindly with my father's household."
>
> JOSHUA 2:9–12

By far the best example of blessing for blessing and cursing for cursing is found in the book of Esther. It is set in the Medo-Persian Empire while the Jews were in captivity and Haman was prime minister under King Ahasuerus (Xerxes). Incensed when Mordecai, a Jew, would not bow down to him, Haman had a 75-foot gallows built for the sheer pleasure of watching this "rebel" hang. And to top it off, he got the king to sign into law a decree ordering the death of all Jews. As the book of Esther records, because of Haman's desire to punish the Jews, God reversed the curse (Esther 7:10). It was Haman who swung from the end of his own rope.

Where are the mighty peoples who mistreated the Jewish people through the ages? The Roman Empire? The Ottomans? The Nazis? A country-by-country tally would show the rise and fall of those who dared touch the apple of God's eye. Since ancient times, the existence and blessing of the Jewish people remain a testimony to the faithfulness of God.

Matthew 25:31–40 reports Jesus' message about the final blessing at the end of this age. When the Son of Man returns, He will gather all nations before Him and separate them the way a herdsman separates sheep from goats. The basis for this separation will be the treatment the nations gave Jesus. Did they feed Him when He was hungry? Did they clothe Him when He was naked? Did they visit Him in prison?

The righteous ones will be confused:

> "Lord, when did we see You hungry, and feed You, or thirsty, and give You drink? And when did we see You a stranger, and invite

You in, or naked, and clothe You? And when did we see You sick, or in prison, and come to You?"

MATTHEW 25:37–39

Jesus explained that His identification with His people is so close that behavior toward them is received in a very personal way:

"Truly I say to you, to the extent that you did it to one of these brothers of Mine, even the least of them, you did it to Me."

MATTHEW 25:40

Some interpret *these brothers of Mine* to be referring exclusively to Christians. But given the "blessing/cursing" concept so well established in Scripture, and the context of the passage, perhaps it is the Jews that the Messiah is specifically referring to. Certainly Jews should at least be *included* in Jesus' remark. Remember, although He did die for all mankind, He had a particular burden for His own brethren according to the flesh. Surely, He would not suddenly change His Father's policy on how to treat the Jews.

In 1980 I had the privilege of preaching in one of those California mega-churches. As is my general custom, I asked the pastor how things were going in his congregation. I was particularly interested in knowing what he believed was responsible for such incredible growth!

"Barry," he confessed, "we were always operating in the red, spending more than we took in. It wasn't until I made a commitment to follow the scriptural admonition to care for Jesus' brethren that the Lord began to bless us. Ever since we began to invite a Jewish missionary to address us at the beginning of each year and to support Jewish missions, we have been operating in the black, *never once* showing a deficit. That's why we've got you here on this first Sunday in January!" More evidence that God keeps His promise to bless those who bless the Jews.

Let me reiterate. God, *whatever* His purposes were, chose to use the Jews as a sort of testing ground. My fellow Jewish people and I were not chosen because we are better than anyone else. Rather, we were chosen to exhibit to the world the grace and faithfulness of God.

"For you are a holy [set-apart] people to the Lord your God; the Lord your God has chosen you to be a people for His own possession out of all the peoples who are on the face of the earth."

DEUTERONOMY 7:6

God cares greatly for His chosen people, so much so that He was willing to sacrifice the best Jew who ever lived to make atonement. If God would do this much for His people, it follows that He would shower great blessings on those who love and care for them as well. That is His will.

The saying goes, "Don't mess with Mother Nature." Even better: "Don't mess with Father God, *or* with His chosen children."

While the greatest blessing you can bring to a Jewish person is the Messiah, there is much opposition to telling Jewish people about Jesus. It is good to remember what the Scripture says about this important endeavor. At times when you encounter resistance, when your best intentions meet with rebuff, that's when you'll want to recall all that God has promised about witnessing to Jews.

Keep in mind that caring for the Jewish people was a hallmark of the heroes of our faith. Remember that bringing Jewish people into the Kingdom is a good investment for eternity. Remember that your neighbor might just be part of the remnant. And, finally, keep in mind that God promises to bless you if you will bless your Jewish friend by introducing him or her to the Messiah.

Now that this is clear in your mind, let me anticipate a question you may have. I hear it often when I speak in churches:

"O.K. I want to see Jewish people saved, but isn't that the work of professional missionaries to the Jews? Can I, a Gentile, *really* play a role in telling Jewish people about Jesus?"

My unequivocal answer to you is *yes*!

# 2

# The Gentiles' Role in Jewish Evangelism
## —or—
## *Provoke 'em to Jealousy!*

During the late 1960s I was faced with a tough decision. The Vietnam War was raging. The draft lottery was operating. My number was low.

I decided to fulfill my military obligation by joining the United States Coast Guard Reserves. After six months of active duty, I was assigned to a Reserve Unit in Washington, D.C., committing me to serve one weekend a month.

One of the more distasteful tasks I had to perform was "swabbing the deck." It wasn't that the work was so hard, but that the floor had just been cleaned by the "regulars" before their weekend leave. I felt indignant that I had to clean a perfectly clean floor. Clearly, this was busywork.

One of my buddies shared this insulting job with me, but it was obvious that he did not share my bad attitude toward it. While I mumbled and grumbled, moaned and groaned, my buddy Loren had the *chutzpah* (Yiddish for "nerve") to whistle and sing! It drove me crazy. After all, wasn't I the one who, through transcendental meditation, was learning to achieve inner peace and relaxation?

One day I had had enough.

"Loren," I said, "what is it about you that makes you so [blankety-blank] happy?" My language had become somewhat salty in my six months of active duty.

Loren's response was simple, but it changed my life. Smiling, he said, "Your Messiah lives in my heart!"

"My Messiah? What's *my* Messiah doing in *your* heart?" I yelled in a not-too-peaceful manner. Then I thought a moment. "And besides," I asked, "who *is* my Messiah?"

Loren explained to me that Jesus was the Messiah sent first to my people, the Jews. If I accepted Him into my life, I would find peace. Real peace.

I was jealous. He seemed to have something real, something worthwhile. Whatever it was, I certainly was not getting it through T.M. And although I wasn't about to make a hasty decision about Jesus without some serious study, Loren had planted a seed of desire within my soul. And that desire eventually found fulfillment in the Person of Jesus.

In Romans, Paul again asks rhetorically,

I say then, Have they [the Jews] stumbled that they should fall? God forbid: but rather through their fall salvation is come unto the Gentiles, for to provoke them to jealousy.

ROMANS 11:11, KJV

In the Torah, the five books of Moses, the Lord told Israel that He would "make them jealous with those who are not a people" (Deuteronomy 32:21). Paul quoted this verse in Romans 10:19 to explain God's approach for reaching His people. He would accomplish this through the nations, the Gentiles.

It came true in my life as it has in the lives of many Jewish people who have received the Messiah through the testimony of a non-Jewish believer. Many have been "provoked to jealousy" by a people who are not even a people.

You are familiar with Matthew 28:19, commonly called the Great Commission: "Go therefore and make disciples of all the nations, baptizing them in the name of the Father and the Son and the Holy Spirit." Often quoted when missionaries are sent out, this verse is appropriate and motivational. But remember, this Commission was not spoken to Gentiles. It was given by Jesus to a handful of Jews.

They were told to fulfill their calling as Jews. Beginning with Jerusalem (Luke 24:47) they were to share the message first with the Jews, and then with all the "nations" of the world, that is, the Gentiles, and make disciples out of them. And since you are most likely reading this book somewhere outside of Jerusalem, we can safely assume that the work those apostles began nearly 2,000 years ago has indeed been effective.

The Great Commission was given directly to Jews, but I believe God has a commission for Gentiles as well, one that many Gentiles who witness to Jewish people have used effectively. I call it "the Gentile Great Commission." You've just been reading about it: "Provoke the Jews to jealousy!"

About this time you might be asking yourself, "Isn't making

people jealous a pretty nasty way for a believer to behave?" Perhaps
it just doesn't sound right to you. But Paul wasn't suggesting that
you adopt a holier-than-thou or condescending attitude. He wasn't
advising Gentiles to put on airs or act superior toward Jews. In fact,
he spoke to the church at Rome about the importance of having a
proper perspective toward Jews:

> Now if their [the Jews'] transgression be riches for the world and
> their failure be riches for the Gentiles, how much more will their
> fulfillment be!
>
> ROMANS 11:12

Paul is commenting on the fact that the transgression or turning
away of the Jewish people from the Gospel hastened the arrival of
the Gospel among the Gentiles. Paul told his Jewish hearers, for
instance, "It was necessary that the word of God should be spoken
to you [the Jews] first; since you repudiate it . . . behold, we are
turning to the Gentiles" (Acts 13:46). If this transgression by the
Jews, therefore, meant life for the Gentiles, how much more the
world will be blessed in that fulfillment!

In other words, believers should look forward to the day when
the Jewish people will experience fulfillment in the Messiah. What
a blessing it will be when Messiah's Body of believers is once again
brimming with Jews!

In his discussion of the olive tree in Romans 11, Paul further
cautioned the church at Rome to regard the unbelieving Jewish
people with a proper attitude. He described all Jewish people as the
natural branches of an olive tree and the Gentiles as wild branches.

Remember that down through the centuries, while the Jews
were being "entrusted with the oracles of God" (Romans 3:1–2), the
Gentiles were pagans. They worshiped idols, sacrificed children,
practiced pagan rituals, and believed a wealth of superstitions.
Then, at their acceptance of the Messiah, Gentiles were "grafted in"
among the natural branches of the olive tree.

Here, Paul warned them that even though they were now part of
the tree, and even though some natural branches had been broken off
because of unbelief (verse 20), the Gentiles in the church were not
to consider themselves superior to those Jews who did not yet

believe. Those Jews still represented the "root" of the tree, which God had cultivated for almost 2,000 years. He told them:

> Do not be arrogant toward the [natural] branches; but if you are arrogant, remember that it is not you who supports the root, but the root supports you. . . . For if you were cut off from what is by nature a wild olive tree, and were grafted contrary to nature into a cultivated olive tree, how much more shall these who are the natural branches be grafted into their own olive tree? For I do not want you, brethren, to be uninformed of this mystery, lest you be wise in your own estimation, that a partial hardening has happened to Israel until the fulness of the Gentiles has come in.
>
> ROMANS 11:18, 24–25

Paul's purpose is to teach Gentiles the proper attitude. God never "unchose" His chosen people. Even when they disobeyed Him—as they did frequently—He still cherished them as His own and sought to lead them to repent. "For the gifts and the calling of God are irrevocable" (verse 29).

Elsewhere Paul wrote that the Jewish people are

> Israelites, to whom belongs the adoption as sons and the glory and the covenants and the giving of the Law and the temple service and the promises, whose are the fathers, and from whom is the Christ [Messiah] according to the flesh, who is over all, God blessed forever. Amen.
>
> ROMANS 9:4–5

The blessings of the Jewish heritage and their special calling to carry out God's purpose have never changed. The gifts with which God has equipped His people for His purpose have contributed to the good of the whole world.

With an attitude of humility and gratitude in order to provoke godly jealousy, you, a Gentile, may have an even more effective witness to Jewish people than many Jewish believers. You can help your Jewish neighbor long for the peace and inner happiness you have. I know it worked to draw me to Jesus. It works for others, too.

# 3

# Anti-Semitism and the Church
## —or—
## *"Christians" Are Not Always Friendly Neighbors*

Not only do Gentiles have a place in Jewish evangelism; Jewish people almost *expect* believers to try to evangelize them. Jews know about Billy Graham, having occasionally bumped into one of his crusades while watching TV. Evangelism is seen as expected behavior for a Christian, so offense is not always taken.

One thing you must keep in mind, however, when witnessing to Jews is the horrendous history of "Christian"/Jewish relations. It has become rather difficult for Jewish people to distinguish the real Jesus through a filter of nearly 2,000 years of persecution perpetrated upon Jews in His name.

This chapter will review, briefly, some of the horrors that have happened to God's chosen people in the name of Jesus. It is not my intention to place a "guilt trip" on the Church. Nor am I implying that the twentieth-century Christian is responsible for the atrocities perpetrated on Jews by those who may not have been Christians. Rather, I want you to become familiar with the poor track record of "Christian"/Jewish relations in order to help you to appreciate the defensive posture your Jewish friend might assume as you attempt to assure him of the love of Jesus.

The small town in Maryland where I grew up was, in many ways, a microcosm of the entire United States. We had a Little League for us youthful baseball players. There was a community pool. Everyone attended the dazzling Fourth of July celebrations. While some cities tend to form natural boundaries dividing the black neighborhood from the Italian section, or the Irish block from the Jewish area, our city was a spicy potpourri, a mixture of all kinds of people coexisting peacefully.

Because of this unusual blend, many of my friends were non-Jews. Some were Protestants, some were Catholics. It never seemed to matter much. What was really important was who hit the baseball the farthest!

Until my Bar Mitzvah.

Jewish boys, at the age of thirteen, go through a ceremony known as Bar Mitzvah, literally "Son of the Commandment." You stand before the synagogue, read from the Scripture, give a speech, and assume your position as an "adult" in the Jewish community. A Bar Mitzvah is no small thing; it requires years of preparation.

Several days a week, prior to the date of my Bar Mitzvah, I had to leave baseball practice early in order to spend time with the rabbi. To study Hebrew. To compose and rehearse my speech. To prepare to chant my assigned portion of the Scripture. My friends didn't appreciate the significance of this important rite and they let their resentment show. It gave me my first taste of anti-Semitism.

It was hard for me to believe, but one afternoon my best friend, Kenny, began to taunt me in front of the other guys. "Barry's going to 'Heeb-Jew' lessons." His words stung. There was derision in his voice. Other boys began to murmur that their dads had told them we Jews had killed Christ. It was the most unpleasant moment in my life.

That kind of prejudice is merely the residue of two millennia of "Christian" anti-Semitism. Anti-Semitism that would make any true believer in Jesus sick! Sadly, you, as a Christian, stand in the shadow of those years.

Later we will discuss what you can do to defuse some of the tension that has arisen between Jews and "Christians." Remember, I bring this history up now to help you understand what is often in the back of the mind of your Jewish friend when he or she starts to hear about the love of Jesus the Christ, Yeshua the Messiah.

## The Jews and the Roman Empire

How would you feel if you were informed that you could no longer salute the American flag? If you were forbidden to have a Christmas tree? If the opinions expressed in your Bible commentaries were publicly denigrated and those books burned? If you were no longer allowed to worship God as you chose?

And how would you feel about those who enforced these restrictions?

This is not a make-believe scenario. These were the kinds of laws enacted and enforced by the Roman government and later the Roman Catholic Church.

When the true Church began, nearly all of its members were Jews. They didn't see themselves as starting a new religion. In fact, they could hardly figure out what to do with the Gentiles who wanted to join in the worship of the Messiah.

The Acts of the Apostles records "great dissension and debate" concerning those who were turning to Jesus "from among the Gentiles" (Acts 15:1–21). Known as the Jerusalem Council, the leaders of the early Church hotly debated whether or not Gentiles who believed in Jesus had to follow the Law of Moses and be circumcised. This concern certainly underscores the Jewishness of the early Church.

But as time passed, Jewish believers became more and more separated from the Jewish community. When the believers fled Jerusalem before the destruction of the Temple, heeding the prophetic warnings of Jesus (see Matthew 24), the split was emphasized. At the Council of Yavneh (70–90 C.E.) a malediction concerning the "sectarians," the Jewish believers in Jesus, was written. It was a prayer for the disappearance of these Jews from the synagogue. Then in 134 C.E.* Jewish believers opposed their Jewish leaders by refusing to participate in the Bar Kokhba revolt. He was being hailed as the Messiah so they couldn't follow him.

The split became a chasm. Jewish believers in Jesus, seen as traitors, were further separated from the fellowship of the Jewish community.

As this separation between the believers and the Jewish community was widening, Rome began to restrict Jewish forms of worship and identity. Those in the Jewish community were called "superstitious" because they believed in a God they could not see. They were also labeled as haters of humanity when they would not participate in pagan ceremonies so prevalent in the Roman Empire. Since much of the public celebration in Rome was imbued with religious significance, Jews were also called unpatriotic because they

---

* Instead of using the initials A.D., which stand for the Latin *Anno Domini*, "year of our Lord," I have chosen to use C.E., standing for "Common Era," as Jews refer to this same period. Because Jewish people, for the most part, have not accepted Jesus as Lord, it is difficult for them to use the letters A.D. I will use B.C.E, "Before the Common Era," instead of B.C., "Before Christ" for dates before the Messiah was born. This will sensitize you toward talking with Jewish people.

would not join in. For example, in Egypt, which was part of the Roman Empire, the story of God's judgment upon Pharaoh was changed. It was said, rather, that Jews were lepers who had been expelled from Egypt.

A tremendous struggle ensued between Judaism, that is, the way of life of the Jews, and Hellenism, the way of life of the Romans (and their predecessors, the Greeks). In order to do away with the Jewish people as a distinct entity, the emperor, Hadrian, forbade circumcision, Sabbath observance, Jewish holidays, the rabbinical academies, the study of Torah (the five books of Moses), and more.

Even though the Romans discouraged the practice of Judaism, somehow the Jews remained intact as a people.

You will hear that it was the study of Torah and Talmud (the codified writings of the rabbis) that kept the Jewish people together. Perhaps God used this, for in an almost miraculous way, the Roman emperor Vespasian permitted Jochanan ben Zakkai, a famous Pharisee of the first century, to start a seminary in Yavneh, which later became the center of Jewish learning.

So during the early rule of the Roman Empire, we see a separation between the Jewish believers and the Jewish community, pressure on all Jews to adopt the Roman way of life, and a struggle to express Jewish identity in the form of scholarship, rather than statehood and Temple worship. This laid the foundation for the anti-Jewish attitudes seen in the next centuries.

It should be mentioned that there were many Jewish believers living in the Roman Empire, as well as many Jewish unbelievers, during this period. Many of the Jewish believers were prominent church leaders.

## The Jews and Later Roman Rule

Many Gentiles living in the Roman Empire adopted "Christianity" when the Emperor Constantine (306–337) declared it to be the state religion. Few in the Church objected to some of the new traditions Constantine instituted. By the 400s, Jews could no longer seek converts. Jews could not have non-Jewish slaves. The "Church" forbade intermarriage and discouraged contact between Christians and Jews. Some of the Church leaders, ostensible followers of the Jew, Jesus, began to preach against His Jewish people.

These actions met with little Church resistance since one of the second-century Church fathers, Justin Martyr, had already laid the foundation for anti-Semitism. He had accused the Jews of inciting Romans to kill Christians. Origen, who died in 251 c.e., accused the Jews of plotting to murder Christians. Even John Chrysostom (344–407 c.e.), known as "the bishop with the golden tongue," called the Jews worthless, greedy, assassins of Christ, and worshipers of the devil. He stated from the pulpit that there could never be forgiveness for the Jews and that it was "incumbent" on Christians to hate them. Jerome, a contemporary of Chrysostom and translator of the Latin Vulgate, devoted one of his celebrated essays entirely to anti-Jewish propaganda. He wrote, "God hates the Jews, and I hate the Jews." Ironic that it was a rabbi who taught him Hebrew.

With this kind of ecclesiastical support, other anti-Jewish changes were made. Sunday, the day that commemorated the resurrection, became the Sabbath day. *Passover* became *Easter*, taking the name of a pagan goddess, Ishtar. Fertility rites soon clouded the truth of the resurrection. In general, what was then known as Christianity ignored the Jewish people, except to persecute them.

The Roman Catholic Church, seeing itself as the new Israel, and, therefore, the new "chosen people," prohibited many Jewish customs. Observance of Passover was forbidden. The reading of the Talmud was outlawed and many priceless, hand-copied works were burned. Invoking the new laws of the Roman government, the state church did all it could to destroy the identity of the Jews, driving God's people further and further away from their own Messiah.

## The Jews and the Second Millennium

Everyone has heard of the Crusades.

In the eleventh and twelfth centuries, a new program was carried out, begun under the orders of Pope Urban II. He promised forgiveness and guaranteed entrance to Paradise to those "Christians" who participated in his plan. Under it, thousands of Crusaders, children included, marched to the Holy Land to deliver it from the infidels, the Muslims who lived there. The intention of the Crusaders was to drive the Mohammedans from the sacred soil of Jesus' homeland. In their religious zeal, they enlisted many not-so-religious people, fortune-hunters, people of low standing looking for some adventure, serfs looking for freedom.

Picture a long parade of soldiers, faces set with determination, prepared for "holy battle." And what do they carry for their standard? The cross, symbol of loyalty to their Lord.

Tragically for the Jews, the Crusaders decided they could start defending "Christianity" right at home. They didn't have to go all the way to Israel to get rid of infidels. Jews, people who opposed what they understood to be "Christianity," lived right there among them. Soon, "Kill a Jew and save your soul!" became the battle cry of the zealous Crusaders.

Later, when the Crusaders arrived in Israel, we hear the story of their encountering a synagogue. Armed with indignation leveled sharply at Jewish unbelief, the Crusaders rounded up the Jews in Jerusalem, herded them into the synagogue, and burned the building to the ground. Marching triumphantly around the inferno, they sang a hymn of praise to God—"Christ, We Adore Thee." Inside the burning synagogue, Jews heard these strains of "Christian" worship as they perished. One wonders how that same Christ regarded those who claimed to "adore" Him as they tortured His brothers.

It didn't get much better in the Roman Catholic-dominated Middle Ages. As frequently happened to the Jews, they were not allowed certain privileges, particularly the privilege of owning land or pursuing certain professions. Because of this, the Jews often held unpopular professions such as tax-collecting. The stereotype of the money-grabbing Jew was being etched into history.

Further, Jews were accused of causing many of the ills that befell the people of this age. They were held responsible for the Black Death or Black Plague of 1348, which killed a huge portion of Europe's population. It was rumored that Jews poisoned the wells. The Jews were also accused of causing many natural disasters like the Lisbon earthquake. They were even charged with killing Christian children to get blood for *matzah*, the unleavened bread of Passover. The Roman Catholic Church laid the death of Jesus upon Jews for all time, eternally charging them with deicide.

In the 1400s the Catholic Church tried another approach in dealing with the Jews. The Jewish population of Spain was offered a choice: Convert to Catholicism or die. Many chose to die rather than follow those they saw as responsible for the deaths and destruction of so many other Jews. Although the Roman Pope tried to stop this action, the Spanish Inquisition remains another indelible black mark on the history of the Church and an enormous roadblock between the Jewish people and the name of Jesus. To this day, during the holy day of Yom Kippur, the Day of Atonement, Jews chant a special prayer dating back to this time. It is a lament called *Kol Nidre*, "All Vows." It was inserted into the liturgy of Yom Kippur because of the Spanish Inquisition. *Kol Nidre* became a cry to nullify the confessions of "Christian" faith uttered by those who had claimed conversion to Catholicism under duress. These people were known as Marranos.

I wish I could say that in the Protestant Reformation anti-Semitism disappeared, but that is not the case.

Martin Luther, the great reformer, although first expressing great respect for the Jews, turned against them in his later years. Frustrated by the lack of Jewish conversions, he wrote that the root of their resistance to the Gospel was their evil nature. He accused the Jews of being ritual murderers, incapable of being saved. He urged the destruction of all Jewish synagogues as well as religious books such as the Talmud. Toward the end of his life, he said that since Jews would not convert, "we ought not to suffer them or bear with them any longer." It is true that he later repented of many of his statements against the Jews, but, once before the public, those words were used against the nation of Israel again and again.

The Russian Orthodox Church, too, like so many other "followers" of Jesus, contributed to the campaign against Jewish people. Many Jews died in the pogroms at the hands of Russian soldiers, called "Cossacks," in the early part of this century. Why were they killed? For one reason only: because they were Jewish.

You may have seen the movie *Fiddler on the Roof*. Remember the violent raid that ruined the joy of the Jewish wedding celebration? And later, the orders given to the Jewish people to leave their little village, the only way of life they had ever known. Destruction and deportation were both common policies toward Jews in Czarist Russia. Many American Jews today are children or grandchildren of those who were beaten and expelled from Russia while the "Church" stood idly by. I'm one of them.

The Germany of World War II was mostly Catholic and Lutheran. In the writings of these "Church" fathers and leaders of "Christianity," the Nazis found much justification for their atrocities.

I hesitate even to utter Jesus' name in the same sentence with the name Adolf Hitler, the one who ordered the torturous destruction of 6,000,000 Jews. Their teachings, after all, were diametrically opposed. Jesus taught love and compassion. Hitler taught hate. But I use the two together to make a point: Jewish people often confuse Christianity with the anti-Semitism of Nazism.

To illustrate this confusion let me share a personal story with you.

In 1975 my wife, Steffi, and I were married. Within a year we were assigned to open an outreach office in Skokie, a suburb of Chicago, to share the Good News with the many Jewish people living there. We were serving at the time with the organization "Jews for Jesus." During that same period, a local Nazi group planned a demonstration in Skokie, which was home to many concentration camp survivors. You may remember *Skokie*, a made-for-TV movie, portraying the events and the conflict that ensued because of this demonstration.

Next door to our storefront office was a kosher butcher. My wife would often buy meat from him. We had developed a casual, pleasant relationship.

During this time of tension in Skokie, I remember going into his shop, looking for an opportunity to talk about the Messiah. After awhile, when we were all alone, the butcher called me aside. I became excited thinking that perhaps we had gotten somewhere in our witness to him.

Rolling up his shirtsleeve, he pointed to a number tattooed across his forearm, the number he had received in a concentration camp in Poland during the Second World War. Then he whispered in a voice seething with bitterness and pain, "This is why I cannot believe in your Jesus!" Somehow he confused Nazism with Christianity.

It was apparent that we had to do something for our people as the time for the Nazi march approached. We had to let them know that true Christianity and Nazi anti-Semitism were totally opposed beliefs.

I gathered together our small staff and a few volunteers and asked if they would join us in a demonstration in front of the Nazi headquarters on the south side of Chicago. Our purpose was to make a clear statement to the Jewish people that true Christians abhor Nazism. After much prayer, agreement was unanimous and we set out to plan the demonstration. Although I usually shy away from this kind of confrontation, we felt compelled to make a statement.

We created colorful placards bearing slogans like "Nazism is anti-Christian," "Jesus was not a Nazi," and "Jesus is the Messiah." Alerting both the media (in order to make the statement) and the police department (in order to keep the peace), we drove down to the Nazi headquarters and held an orderly, legal demonstration in front of their building.

Notifying the police had been a smart thing to do. Right in the middle of our demonstration, the Nazis dramatically threw open their heavy garage doors and stood menacingly in closed ranks, brandishing large guns across their chests. I could feel my heart pound as the sweat began to pour. But we kept praying and standing our ground.

TV cameras came to film the event, but as soon as they left, the police advised us to leave the area to avoid a serious problem. Our goal had been accomplished. Our statement would be made. That evening, the media reported on the demonstration; articles were published that told our story. After that, many Jewish people living in Skokie came by our office to thank us for taking so public a stand against the Nazis. Even the butcher seemed friendlier.

Those of us in Jewish ministry are sometimes told that our efforts are worse than those of Hitler. "The Nazis destroyed Jewish bodies, but *you* destroy Jewish souls," we are told. Naturally, to be misunderstood hurts. But we cannot deny the Messiahship of Jesus even if it hurts. Jewish parents are often crushed when their children accept Jesus. Spouses, too, go through their share of grief over one who professes belief in the Messiah.

We knew we couldn't erase the pain of those who had been through the concentration camps. But the eyes of many in Skokie saw that true Christians would stand up against Nazism. Testimonies such as this one go a long way toward overcoming 2,000 years of poor Christian/Jewish relations. There are thousands of testimonies of true believers who stood with the Jews in Nazi Germany, risking and sometimes losing their lives to protect and hide them. Corrie ten Boom's *The Hiding Place* is a wonderful statement of how a true Christian feels about the Jewish people. It's worth reading and even sharing with your Jewish neighbor.

You might be asking yourself just why there is confusion about this in the first place. Why should Jewish people make a connection between Christianity and Nazism? To begin with, Adolf Hitler was born into a Catholic family. Since Jewish people are born Jewish, they automatically assume that Hitler was born Christian.

Furthermore, many in the Nazi party faithfully attended church. Observing the Nazis on the weekend, and then watching what they did during the week, many Jewish people raised the logical question, "If their church preached love, how could these church-going people preach hate?" The false conclusion they reached was that anti-Semitism was somehow part of Christian teaching. Unfortunately, sometimes churches did teach this.

Granted, churches nowadays don't teach persecution of Jews, but I have sat in large evangelical churches and heard comments and remarks that revealed latent anti-Semitic attitudes. Like the time I heard one preacher lambaste "those self-righteous, hypocritical Pharisees!" He neglected to state that the unrighteous behavior he spoke of was possibly the exception, not necessarily the rule. He also forgot to mention those Pharisees who became followers of Jesus.

Jews, with good reason, are very sensitive toward anti-Semitic innuendo.

If you're going to be effective in your witness, you'll need to recognize the perceptions of your Jewish neighbor. As kind as you are, as honest and decent and neighborly as you have been, you must also understand that the memory of these unforgettable atrocities will be ever-present in his or her mind. Although you don't carry the sword of the Crusader, although you are not offering the ultimatum of the Inquisitor, although you do not spout the anti-Jewish diatribe of a Nazi, you are still identified as one of "them"—a non-Jew. A potential anti-Semite.

Jewish people often classify the world into "us" and "them." Jews have learned that given the right degree of pressure, the right amount of propaganda, and the right kind of preparation, almost anyone is capable of persecuting a Jewish scapegoat. Jews have been warned by those who have lived through the Holocaust, "Remember, it *can* happen again."

As a word of encouragement to you, know that you really can overcome "Church" history through an honest, open, loving friendship with your Jewish neighbor.

In the next chapter you will learn how to make yourself more credible to your Jewish neighbor so that you might be more effective in your witness. You can become considered one of "us," no longer one of "them."

# 4

# How to Have a More Credible Witness

—or—

*Being a Little Jewish Wouldn't Hurt!*

Remember the old TV show *Dragnet?* Joe Friday would always insist when he questioned a suspect, "The facts, ma'am, just give me the facts." We'd all like to believe we make our decisions based on the facts alone. But it is simply not true.

If it were true, dealers wouldn't promote automobiles by using provocative women or handsome men. Advertisers wouldn't sell their products with catchy jingles or upbeat video effects. Candidates wouldn't spend millions of campaign dollars on marketing people hired to improve their "images." Persuasion doesn't always occur just because of facts.

Often, what really reaches us is a salesman's personality, a candidate's "charisma," or a preacher's presence. Facts are sometimes secondary.

This ability to influence another is often called "credibility." We might hear two speakers saying precisely the same thing, but one will have greater impact on us than the other. If the scripts are the same, that difference in impact can be attributed to the speaker's credibility. Somehow we perceive him as more believable, more trustworthy, more reliable.

Credibility sometimes is looked at as some sort of "God-given gift." Some say you're either born with it or you're not. Social scientists who have studied credibility draw different conclusions: It can be attained. In other words, for our purposes, there are things you can do to help you become more credible in your Jewish neighbor's eyes.

One finding from communication research is that credibility bears directly upon attitude change and persuasion. A person who is perceived as having greater credibility will bring about more attitude change and persuasion in a listener than one who is not. We experience this in our lives daily.

How do certain teachers "get more" out of their students? What makes some bosses successful in motivating their employees? Why do certain pastors achieve substantially greater impact on their congregations than others? If the content of the messages is basically the same—learn, work, grow—to what, then, can we attribute the difference in effect? Often the difference is credibility.

People have pondered this phenomenon for centuries. As far back as Plato and Aristotle, credibility has been discussed. In more recent years, experts in communication have delved into the study of credibility, emerging with some valuable insights.

In the late 1960s and early 1970s I taught communications at Howard University in Washington, D.C. Even then, when credibility research was in its first ten or twenty years, dozens of books and hundreds of articles had been written on the subject.

I'd like to mention a few of the conclusions that have been reached in credibility research in order to help us prepare for communicating the Gospel effectively with Jewish people.

Social scientists and communicologists report that credibility is based upon three character traits: trustworthiness, expertness, and identification. Each of these traits can be identified and measured, even though there is some overlap among them. Those perceived as having a high degree of each of these characteristics are usually more effective in persuading others.

## Trustworthiness

Trustworthiness is the trait that enables a person to feel safe with another. It is related to warmth, friendliness, openness. A trustworthy person "doesn't have a mean bone in his body."

Dan Rigney is just such a person. I first met Dan at a special Hebrew-Christian Rosh Hashana service. Rosh Hashana is called the Jewish New Year, the first of the high holy days. At the time we first met, Dan was a missionary with the American Board of Missions to the Jews, now known as Chosen People Ministries. I was not yet a believer, but I was curious about what a Hebrew-Christian service was.

There was Dan, sporting a nice, long, rabbi-like beard and wearing white rabbinical robes. He wore a miter, a white silk head covering commemorative of the priests of ancient Israel. But sticking out from the hem of his robe was something I'd never seen a rabbi wear: cowboy boots! This made an unusual composite, to say the least.

During the service I heard many traditional Hebrew prayers. I also heard many Jewish people giving their testimonies. It didn't take me too long to realize that this was not just a Jewish service that was open to Christians, or a congregation for interfaith marriages (my original assumption); this was a service where both Jews and Gentiles believed in Jesus!

After the service, I went up to Dan in a rather accusatory manner. "You're no Jew!" I charged. "You're just pretending to be a Jew." His warm smile and honest words disarmed me. "No, I'm not Jewish," Dan admitted, "but I love the Jewish people because of Jesus. I'm a grafted-in Gentile."

I no longer felt angry or combative. Dan's sincerity was so real it was almost tangible. Immediately, I found him to be trustworthy, safe, credible. I wanted to know more. I began attending Dan's weekly Bible study where I later met the Messiah.

Trustworthiness is not something that can be trumped up. As we walk in the Messiah's light and become more like Him, we grow toward being totally trustworthy. Growth and maturity naturally yield credibility. The fruit of the Spirit—love, joy, peace, patience, kindness, goodness, faithfulness, gentleness, self-control (Galatians 5:22–23)—all contribute toward making us trustworthy people.

A word of caution. Some individuals buy the lie that no one should be involved in service for the Lord until he or she is perfect. They say, "I'm too big a sinner for anyone to listen to me!"

Nothing could be further from the truth. Paul struggled with the flesh continually, but that didn't stop him from preaching. There is not a preacher, pastor, missionary, or Bible school teacher who is perfect. Yet all trust the Lord to enable them to fulfill God's calling for them.

Likewise, you and I, imperfect as we are, have been called to bring the Good News back to His people, the Jews. Probably we could all be more trustworthy. But God can still use us. The thing to remember is to be honest in your testimony.

Sometimes we believers deny painful realities in an attempt to impress others with our faith. Although we have been granted eternal life in the world to come, living on this earth has its share of disappointments and pain. To deny these feelings is to deny the Lord who has blessed us with a variety of experiences to help us grow. What's more, this denial is misleading to those to whom we are witnessing. They are often more aware of the problems in our lives than we'd like to admit. It's O.K. to tell your Jewish friend about the problems you face. You will actually be more trustworthy, since your Jewish friend probably is already aware of them.

Once, when I was conducting a seminar on sharing the Messiah with Jewish people, one of the participants was experiencing tremendous personal suffering in her life. Divorce, death, depression. When we came to this section on credibility and trustworthiness, she said she felt inadequate to share the Messiah. She decided to wait until all was well in her life. I felt that, to the contrary, it was just then that she should have shared.

Her Jewish friend would have related to her suffering and might have offered to help her. And, what's more important, she could have been like Job who, in the midst of his suffering, affirmed his faith in God and His Messiah: "And as for me, I know that my Redeemer lives, and at the last He will take His stand on the earth" (Job 19:25). Her Jewish friend would have been impressed.

Trustworthiness is an important factor in credibility and credibility is important to good communication and persuasion. We need to let the Lord mold us into the image of our trustworthy Savior; in this way we can be more credible and more persuasive in our witness.

## Expertness

With regard to witnessing to Jewish people, this is the area in which most well-meaning Christians give up. I've heard things like, "How can I talk about the Bible to the people to whom this Book was first given?" or, "I'd love to witness to my Jewish neighbor, but he's too smart for me."

It is true that Jewish people were the ones chosen by God first to receive His holy Word. It is also true that Jewish people highly prize a good education. But today, surprisingly, Jewish people are relatively illiterate when it comes to knowing the Bible, and I don't mean just the New Testament. Most Jews, the vast majority, have never read the Old Testament.

Even those Jewish people who go to synagogue regularly read only certain parts of Scripture. You see, on each Sabbath day only a portion of Scripture is read. Something from the Torah, Genesis through Deuteronomy, and something from the Prophets. A Jewish person who does his Bible reading in synagogue every Saturday will still not have read the entire Old Testament.

What's more incredible, much of the prophetic writing is completely ignored in the synagogues, especially those portions known as Messianic prophecies (this will be discussed at greater length in chapter 6). The average Christian who has gone to church and attended Sunday school is more likely better versed in the Hebrew Scriptures than his Jewish counterpart. You, relatively speaking, are the expert.

Even if you are confronted with a question you are not prepared to answer, be honest. I would prefer a doctor tell me he needed to study or confer about my symptoms rather than fake a diagnosis. Don't be afraid to admit, "I don't know, but I'll look it up and get back to you."

The words of the apostle Peter aptly conclude the subject of expertness. He admonished believers "always [to be] ready to make a defense to every one who asks you to give an account for the hope that is in you, yet with gentleness and reverence" (1 Peter 3:15). That was Peter's way of saying we should increase our expertness, tempering it with trustworthiness, so that we can become more credible witnesses. We are to be a witness to *everyone*. Including your Jewish neighbor.

## Identification

It meant a lot to me that Dan Rigney had taken the trouble to identify with my people by wearing the rabbi's robes and speaking Hebrew. Though I was surprised and perhaps somewhat offended at first, his efforts triggered my curiosity. Then, when I sensed his genuine love for the Jewish people, I was glad he had chosen to make the identification. He desired, as much as possible, to become one of "us."

Likewise, when I've met Christians who enjoy Jewish culture, humor, or literature, it has always made me feel closer to them. Identification is a key ingredient of credibility.

Paul, apostle to the Gentiles, said, "And to the Jews I became as a Jew, that I might win Jews" (1 Corinthians 9:20). Paul was, of course, already Jewish, but he emphasized this Jewishness as he communicated with the Jewish people. He was even willing to take a Nazirite vow (Acts 18:18), something only a religious Jew would do. If you want to win your Jewish friend to the Messiah, it will help to understand his frame of mind. To become more like him. To appreciate the things he regards as special, significant, even sacred.

Identifying with someone will give you greater credibility and enable you to be more persuasive. We are drawn to the political candidate who speaks for us and seems to understand our needs. We relate to the salesman who makes an effort to understand our wants. We even respond to the TV commercial that shows people whose lifestyles mirror our own.

In witnessing to Jewish people, it is indeed possible for a Gentile to identify. In Section III, I'll be discussing some of the characteristics of Jewish people, in generalities, of course. But here, let me say that if you want to be more credible in your witness, become an "us."

Learn what issues concern Jewish people most. You might subscribe to the *Jerusalem Post* or your local Jewish newspaper. Attend some lectures or celebrations sponsored by the local Jewish Community Center or synagogue. You will not only learn about Jewish people, you will also enjoy a personally enriching experience, *and* you will be making an effort to identify.

Experience and enjoy the rich culture of God's chosen people. Understanding Jewish humor is a fun way to get started. Books such as *The Joys of Yiddish* and *A Treasury of Jewish Humor* are thoroughly enjoyable to read and will help you identify with or at least get a feeling for the humor of Jewish people. You may even learn some new jokes.

Jewish music can be fun, worshipful, and soul-stirring. You already hear strains of it hidden within some of the melodies of Barry Manilow, Paul Simon, Marvin Hamlisch, and others. But it's much more. Perhaps you might enjoy going to a concert of Jewish music with your Jewish neighbor.

Literature is terribly important to God's chosen people. Books by Chaim Potok, such as *The Chosen* and *My Name Is Asher Lev,* offer you a keen insight into the New York Orthodox Jewish community, a community that has impacted Jews everywhere. Other writers such as Isaac Bashevis Singer and Sholom Aleichem will teach you about Jewish backgrounds and tradition.

Gastronomics are also important. You might already enjoy bagels (I think one fast food place is offering them for breakfast). This Jewish "hole-y roll" is quickly becoming part of American life. To really identify, try lox—right after payday! Lox, smoked salmon, needs an acquired taste, but as a steady diet it could put a dent in the budget! It's expensive and eaten infrequently.

In the '60s, bagels were still viewed pretty exclusively as a "Jewish" food. Since I considered them a necessary staple in my diet, I would always bring a few dozen bagels back to college after going home for the holidays. Ohio University in Athens, Ohio, didn't know about these odd-looking doughnut-shaped rolls. So it was not long before I'd acquired the nickname *Bagels.*

My friends at college learned to love bagels. One of my fraternity brothers accompanied me home during a spring break. To the honored guest, my mom served lox and bagels for breakfast. Somehow, my Midwestern friend could just not get into it. Lox is a little like sushi, the Japanese raw fish delicacy. But don't worry, you don't really have to eat lox to identify with Jews. Bagels will do fine.

Missionaries to other cultures have finally understood the message of identification. The traditional missionary approach had been to try to get those whom they sought to reach to become just like the folks back home. It became a goal to persuade a tribal native to succumb to the Western custom of wearing a tie. It wasn't just the Gospel the missionaries brought; it was also Western culture.

But in recent years, missionaries have become sensitive to and appreciative of the culture of the people they seek to reach. Learning the native language and customs, today's missionaries encourage the development of indigenous churches. Sometimes called cross-cultural communication, missiologists refer to this practice as *contextualization*, putting the Gospel in the context of the people with whom they are working.

Trustworthiness, expertness, identification are the three foundational blocks upon which credibility is built. And remember, increased credibility generally leads to more effective communication and persuasion.

Your mission, should you decide to accept it, is to grow in these three areas of godliness for your own personal enrichment as well as for the sake of your witness. Remember, yours is not a "mission impossible."

Here in Section I, you've learned some of the reasons for bringing the Gospel to Jewish people and have been challenged to fulfill "the Gentile Great Commission"—*provoke them to jealousy!* You've learned the background of the "us/them" syndrome and the tragedies of "Church"/Jewish history, both of which affect the way Christians are perceived when they witness. And you've learned how to be more credible in your witness.

In the next section on the "Jewish Gospel," we will look at ways to present the Messiah that are both understandable and acceptable to Jewish people. It is critical to understand not only who you are and how you are perceived, but that you learn to communicate in an honest—and Jewish—way.

# SECTION II

## The "Jewish Gospel"

I. YOU:
The Gentile
Christian

II. YOUR MESSAGE:
The "Jewish Gospel"

III. THE AUDIENCE:
Your Jewish
Neighbor

IV. THE FEEDBACK:
Barriers to Belief

Back to our witnessing model.

With increased comprehension about your role in Jewish evangelism, gleaned from Section I, we can now focus our discussion on the message, namely, the "Jewish Gospel."

You might be thinking, "I thought there was only one Gospel. What's all this about a Jewish Gospel?" Good question!

There *is* only one Gospel, just as there is only "one body and one Spirit . . . one Lord, one faith, one baptism, one God and Father of all" (Ephesians 4:4–6). But in this same passage, Paul explains that there is a variety of gifts in ministering the Gospel—apostles, prophets, evangelists, pastors, and teachers (4:11). Likewise, there is a variety of approaches in communicating the message of the Messiah.

This is shown in the effective work done by campus outreaches. InterVarsity, Campus Crusade, Navigators, and others have a particular approach to working with college students. They minister a unique "college student" Gospel. Sometimes, churches are planted near campuses in order to minister specifically to the needs of college students. I saw this ministry in action when I spoke in just such a church planted next to a well-known southern California college.

Whereas most pastors tend to dress rather conservatively—dark suits, ties, wingtip shoes—the pastors of this church wore sport shirts, penny loafers, and Levis. The music in this campus church was played on guitar and had a contemporary sound, quite different from traditional church hymns played on piano or organ.

And unlike many church buildings, architecturally designed to inspire worship and induce awe, this church met in a cozy carpeted room where some sat on folding chairs and others on the floor.

I learned from this very successful campus church that college students can best be reached within their own cultural context. Comfortably cross-legged on that carpet, those young adults were more likely to listen to the Gospel than sitting stiffly in a wooden pew.

The same principle holds true in witnessing to Jewish people. I suppose if those campus pastors were writing a book to help others reach out on the local campus, they might have entitled this section "The 'Campus Gospel,' " hoping to alert the reader to consider approaching college students in a unique and more effective way.

That's why I call this section, "The 'Jewish Gospel.' " Not that Jewish people are saved in a different way from Gentiles, but that the Good News ought to be presented in a fashion that makes it most easily understood by Jewish people. Remember, the Church has not always approached the people of Israel in a very positive, loving way. It's time to try something different, something that just might work.

# 5

## The Good News in the Old Testament
### —or—
### *Gimme That Old Testament Religion!*

My first real encounter with the New Testament took place in a hotel room. It was during a transcendental meditation retreat.

Because I was preparing to become a teacher of T.M., I set out to devour as much of the teaching of the Maharishi as I could. A one-month teacher training retreat in northern California fit right into my plans and those of 1,400 other "seekers of truth," (as we "humbly" referred to ourselves). After this first month of training I continued making plans to go on to Majorca, Spain, for the completion of the course. God, however, had another agenda.

Leaving California and returning home to Washington, D.C., I signed up for a weekend T.M. retreat in the beautiful mountains of Virginia. The retreat included eight, nine, or ten daily meditation sessions instead of the usual two, and I was expecting to break through to "higher consciousness." Something certainly did break through as you will see.

While deep in one of my meditations, I experienced "astral projection" or "soul travel." I sensed that my soul was rising from my body, hovering up near the ceiling. I felt as though I were floating in midair, looking down upon my body sitting on the bed. It felt just as strange as it sounds! I was terrified! I had never before experienced such a supernatural event.

I was experiencing something uncommon and bizarre, and I was scared, so I looked around the room for something to read. Something down-to-earth, to take my mind off of what had just happened. But I couldn't find anything other than T.M. pamphlets, T.M. booklets, and T.M. materials. But there in the night table drawer, I discovered a Gideon Bible.

*This will certainly be a change,* I thought as I opened the book. Being Jewish, I wanted to avoid the New Testament because that was the Bible for the Gentiles. Since Hebrew reads from right to left, Jewish Bibles and prayer books open from what you might call the back.

So I turned to the back of that Bible figuring I'd open to Genesis. Instead I found myself smack in the midst of something mysteriously entitled "The Revelation to John," admittedly an unusual place to begin a Bible study! When I realized that I was in the New Testament, a strange uneasiness swept over me. I had been taught that Jews had no business reading the New Testament. It was a book that spoke about the Gentile god, Jesus. Furthermore, I had never even been permitted to utter the name *Jesus* in my home. I felt certain that I was violating some ancient Jewish law.

Suddenly a passage caught my eye. I found myself in chapter seven, reading about 144,000 Jewish believers in Jesus. They were saying, "Salvation to our God who sits on the throne, and to the Lamb" (verse 10).

"Ha!" I laughed. "I'll believe that when I see it! Jews don't believe in Jesus." Vindicated by my declaration, I tossed that Bible across the room. I felt the subject was closed. (Don't worry, I have had many opportunities to thank the Gideons since becoming a believer!)

For most Jews, the New Testament is considered irrelevant at the least and blasphemous at worst. Although it is possible to lead a Jew to Jesus by quoting exclusively from the New Testament, it is wiser to begin with what is already familiar or at least accepted as Jewish, that is, the Old Testament, the *Tenakh*.

In this chapter, then, I will outline some premises that you can relate to your Jewish neighbor once you have established yourself as a credible friend.

## Premise 1: God Loves the Jewish People

We're all familiar with the carrot-and-stick approach to motivation—reward and punishment. Sometimes both are necessary to get a mule to move, but it certainly seems more humane to try the carrot before resorting to the stick.

The same holds true when dealing with people. A boss can motivate his employees to produce quality work through threats and punishment, but the inducement of reward is more inspiring. A teacher can attempt to lambaste his students into learning, but in the long run, positive reinforcement is more successful. A parent can harass his or her children into obedience and submission, but loving them into the proper relationship promotes better behavior.

When witnessing to the truth of Messiah Jesus, love will go a lot farther than fear. It is true that fear can motivate, but it also promotes a relationship fraught with mistrust and anxiety. On top of this, Jewish people struggle with a sort of generalized guilt.

Exactly where this guilt got started no one knows. Perhaps it has to do with a deep-seated awareness of not fulfilling the expectation of God's Law. Maybe it comes from millennia of nonacceptance by the rest of the world. I don't know for sure. What I do know is that whatever the source, this guilt is a real component of the Jewish psyche today. The first step, then, in presenting the Gospel in the Old Testament is to let Jewish people know that God indeed loves them.

> "The Lord did not set His love on you nor choose you because you were more in number than any of the peoples, for you were the fewest of all peoples, but because the Lord loved you and kept the oath which He swore to your forefathers. . . ."
>
> DEUTERONOMY 7:7–8

There's a cost being chosen, and sometimes it has an expensive pricetag attached. But Jews have learned at least to have a sense of humor about it.

In the movie *Fiddler on the Roof,* Tevye, the papa, takes stock of his life. He has five unmarried daughters, a dry milk cow, poverty aplenty, and to top it off, a more-than-occasional attack from his neighbors, the Cossacks. Considering this inventory, Tevye raises his eyes and looks up to heaven. "I know we are the chosen people, but once in a while can't You choose someone else?"

True as this may seem at times to your Jewish neighbor, still it's important to introduce the fact that he or she was uniquely chosen and is especially loved by God.

## Premise 2: Sin Has Broken the Love Relationship Between God and Israel

"O.K., O.K.," your Jewish neighbor relents, "God chose me and loves me. So kindly explain all the suffering the Jewish people have had to endure. And what about *my* problems, while you're at it?"

We will deal with this and other specific questions in greater detail in Section IV, but here I want to explain to you the second premise in witnessing from the *Tenakh*, the Old Testament.

Most Jewish people today—for that matter, most people in general—have done their best to ignore the question of sin. Psychologists might use terms like *aberrant conduct* or *socially unacceptable behavior*. Some groups, like the T.M. people, discuss stress and strain. Others talk about the relativism of morality.

There is a need to return to the biblical explanation of man's bad behavior, and that explanation is sin, which the Bible describes as having "[fallen] short of the glory of God" (Romans 3:23).

The prophet Isaiah recognized sin to be the problem in Israel's relationship to God:

> Your iniquities have made a separation between you and your God, and your sins have hidden His face from you, so that He does not hear.
>
> ISAIAH 59:2

Without a relationship with God, one cannot experience peace and fulfillment, nor can a person know the love of God. Because of sin, Israel in general and your Jewish neighbor in particular experience broken relationships with a loving God. But in His mercy, God has made a provision.

## Premise 3: God Has a Solution to the Sin Problem

In God's infinite wisdom, He realized that His people would not live up to His standards for them. But in His infinite mercy He made provision for His people's sins:

> "For the life of the flesh is in the blood, and I have given it to you on the altar to make atonement for your souls; for it is the blood by reason of the life that makes atonement."
>
> LEVITICUS 17:11

This is the principle of substitutionary, or vicarious, atonement. The "life for a life" principle. Because of sin, something has to die.

In the Garden of Eden, or, as Jewish people call it, *Gan Eden*, Adam and Eve sinned. Previous to their sin, the Lord God had said,

> "From any tree of the garden you may eat freely; but from the tree of the knowledge of good and evil you shall not eat, for in the day that you eat from it you shall surely die."
>
> GENESIS 2:16–17

Clear from the start, the penalty for disobedience to God's Word was death.

Here, at the beginning of human history, God made plain that it was essential to heed His Word. Humankind, however, failed to listen. God had anticipated that failure and provided a system of substitutionary atonement. Sin exacted a price; that price had to be paid. But in God's plan, a substitute could be provided to cover the penalty for human sin. In the Garden of Eden it was an animal whose life was taken to provide "garments of skin for Adam and his wife" after they sinned (Genesis 3:21). The first human beings' sins were covered by the shedding of blood, in this case, the blood of an animal, literally sacrificed to cover their shame.

Later, God provided an elaborate sacrificial system for His people Israel, anticipating their failure to obey the Mosaic Law. Once again blood was to be shed for the sins of His people. Again: "For the life of the flesh is in the blood, and I have given it to you on the altar to make atonement for your souls . . ." (Leviticus 17:11).

God provided and provided again. Yet the final provision for the sin of Israel and for the world would entail a more costly, more dramatic display of love. At last sin would see ultimate atonement, through the shed blood of the Messiah. This is what is meant when we say that Jesus died for our sins. He provided atonement—at-one-ment—a restored relationship with God.

In a simple form, these three premises provide the basis for presenting the Gospel to your Jewish neighbor from the Old Testament.

- P. mise 1—God loves the Jewish people.
- Premise 2—Sin has broken the relationship between God and Israel.
- Premise 3—God has a solution to the sin problem.

All that is left now is to show how Jesus became the ultimate sacrifice offered by God to provide atonement, reconciliation, and restoration between God and His people, Israel. For this, we need to look at the subject known as Messianic prophecy.

# 6

# Messianic Prophecy
## —or—
## *It Says That in <u>My</u> Bible?*

People love prophecy. Tabloids that flank the supermarket checkout lines announce the predictions of men and women who claim to have the gift of prophecy. Whether these forecasts turn out to be right or wrong, readers are drawn to their predictions and remain titillated by the possibility of supernatural foreknowledge.

In the Bible, God used prophecy to admonish and warn His people about their present sinful behavior. At times prophecy foretold the future. Sometimes it foretold future consequences of Israel's actions. But often prophecy was a message of hope focusing on the coming Messiah.

Could there have been any information more significant for the Israelites than the details of the One yet to come, the One who would rescue Israel from an often desperate situation?

No! Nothing captured the imagination and longing of the Jews more powerfully than the hope of the coming Messiah. God presented His people with a portrait of His anointed One, His Messiah. A portrait painted with the brushstrokes of what we call Messianic prophecy.

Some claim to have discovered as many as 333 Messianic prophecies in the Old Testament. Those who offer Messianic prophecy when witnessing to Jewish people, however, don't usually deal with more than about a dozen. This chapter will highlight the most effective and most commonly used Messianic prophecies so that you may better understand how to incorporate these portions of Scripture when sharing with your Jewish neighbor.

When I conduct seminars in churches, I'm repeatedly asked certain questions. One that invariably crops up is, "If these Messianic prophecies are so clear, why don't the Jewish people believe them, and recognize their Messiah?" The answer may surprise you.

*Most Jewish people have never seen Messianic prophecies.*

"How can this be," I am asked, "when they are right there in the Old Testament?"

While it is true that the prophecies that point to Jesus can be found in the Tenakh, it is also true, as I said before, that most Jews have never read through the Old Testament.

Perhaps a slight digression will be helpful here. In the past, rabbis, in their desire to protect their people from straying, would often prohibit the reading of Christian literature. Due to the tremendous persecution against Jews in the name of Jesus, the leaders of the Jewish people didn't want their flocks to be seduced by what appeared to be an anti-Jewish religion. To ensure loyalty and to prevent curiosity, it appears that Messianic prophecies were deliberately eliminated from the traditional weekly Bible readings.

One can appreciate the intentions of the rabbis. Considering their wish to hold their people together, this protective approach is understandable. They were using the limited light they had. Unfortunately, this approach denied the full Word of God.

Messianic prophecy, then, is something with which very few Jews are familiar. Furthermore, since the doctrine of a Messiah has fallen from prominence in Judaism, mention of Messianic prophecy is omitted from most Jewish religious schools.

It is usually a missionary to the Jews who brings up the question of Messianic prophecy, and these missionaries have been cast in a villainous role, cloaked with a cloud of conversionism and anti-Semitism. The simple fact is, however, that Messianic prophecy was given by God so that we might know about the coming Messiah, that we might await the arrival of our King, and that we might recognize Him at His advent. Prophecy is part of God's Word and will accomplish the purposes for which it was given, namely, to point the Jewish people to Jesus the Messiah.

It is good to know, also, that it is not just Christians who considered these portions of Scripture to be Messianic and predictive in nature. They were considered Messianic by the rabbis of old. The writings of the rabbis often refer to these very same prophecies as Messianic.

Modern-day "Christian" anti-Semitism has persuaded Jewish scholars to attribute other interpretations to some of these passages, but as you witness to your Jewish neighbor, know that history is on your side. Know, too, that the love you show can undo many years of horror perpetrated in the name of Jesus. All over the country, true believers in Jesus break through the horrendous history of Church/ synagogue relations with love, and, armed with Messianic prophecy, they communicate the truth of the Messiah to His people.

## Establishing the Role of the Prophet

Abraham, Isaac, Jacob, Moses, David—these are some of the biblical names with which the Jewish community is most familiar. But Haggai, Zephaniah, Amos, and Micah are not so familiar. Jewish people don't think much about the prophets of Israel.

When prophets are discussed, it's usually within the context of social reform, not unlike discussing the many Jews involved in social reform in the world today. But the prophets of ancient Israel performed another important role.

They were not just men chosen to call the people of Israel back to God; they were often selected to convey some very important future events.

The Lord created the office of prophet and described it specifically in the Torah:

> "I will raise up a prophet from among their countrymen like you, and I will put My words in his mouth, and he shall speak to them all that I command him. And it shall come about that whoever will not listen to My words which he shall speak in My name, I Myself will require it of him."
>
> DEUTERONOMY 18:18–19

The office of prophet was established because the children of Israel could not bear to hear the voice of God directly. If a person spoke in the name of God, but was not really a prophet, he was to die:

> "But the prophet who shall speak a word presumptuously in My name which I have not commanded him to speak, or which he shall speak in the name of other gods, that prophet shall die."
>
> DEUTERONOMY 18:20

The test for authenticity hinged upon the accuracy of the prediction:

"When a prophet speaks in the name of the Lord, if the thing does not come about or come true, that is the thing which the Lord has not spoken. The prophet has spoken it presumptuously; you shall not be afraid of him."

DEUTERONOMY 18:22

True prophets foretold future events because God wanted His people to know about them. For Israel, nothing was more important than the coming Messiah. Who would He be? How would He come? Where would He be born? When would He arrive? What, finally, would He do?

## Some Useful Messianic Prophecies

### Isaiah 53: The Suffering Servant

Without question, the Messianic prophecy that has had the greatest effect on Jewish people has been Isaiah 53. I remember vividly the day I first was shown the portrait of the sinless Suffering Servant of God whom I suspected at once to be Jesus.

I had been regularly attending a Bible study conducted by Dan Rigney, the missionary with the cowboy boots. Dan was teaching from the book of Isaiah.

Working our way through the prophet, we read about sin. Intellectually, I was ignorant about sin; experientially, I had begun to feel more and more convicted about the sin in my life. Even without completely understanding or accepting the standards of God's Law, the Word of God was having its way in my heart.

One night at the Bible study, Dan opened his Bible and asked us to turn to Isaiah 53. There before me was a vivid description of Someone who would give His life to atone for the sins of His people. Following the lesson Dan asked me for my comments. "That was nice," I remarked coolly, "and I'd love to believe it, but you've obviously taken some New Testament portion and stuck it in the Old Testament. Anyone can see that those verses are talking about Jesus!"

I turned to the front of the Bible and pointed to where it indicated this was the King James Version of Scripture. "I'll just have to check out those verses in my own Jewish Bible." But where *was* my Bible? I hadn't seen it since the day of my Bar Mitzvah.

I drove over to my parents' home, trotted down the steps to the basement, and found my old Bible on the top of the bookshelf. Reaching up, I removed it from the shelf, blew off the dust, and hunted for Isaiah 53. There, to my shock, I found *the very same words* I had read in the Christian Bible. What felt like a bolt of lightning went through me as I realized Jesus *was* the One of whom Isaiah had spoken.

My parents and several of their friends were upstairs enjoying a dinner party. Taking the steps two at a time, I waved my open Bible and cried, "I've found the Messiah!" *Strange,* I thought. No one seemed to appreciate the significance of my discovery. In fact, from the look on everyone's face, I think I may have ruined the dinner party.

But I was now convinced that Jesus was the Messiah. It had been Isaiah 53 that really got to me.

When you read Scripture's classic description of the Suffering Servant, you see a man going quietly to His death in order to pay for the sins of His people. You watch a man die with criminals, yet be buried with the rich. One who would be sinless yet bear the sins of many, performing an intercessory role. You see a man whom the Lord was pleased to sacrifice as a guilt offering, One who would see His seed after His death. It is a picture of the life, death, and resurrection of Jesus, the Messiah.

In ancient times, the rabbis taught that this portion of Scripture spoke of the Messiah. Having heard enough about a Messiah who would die and then reign as King, they went so far as to offer a two-Messiah theory to explain the dual role the Messiah would have. *Mashiach ben Yoseph* (Messiah, son of Joseph) and *Mashiach ben David* (Messiah, son of David) were the names given to these "two" Messiahs.

The first, in the likeness of Joseph, Jacob's beloved son who was sold into slavery by his jealous brothers, would bear the sins of His people. The second, in the spirit of King David, would reign over Israel. Isaiah 53 was the portion used to explain the sacrificial role of the Messiah. And, as we will see in a moment, the prophet Zechariah foretold His rule as King.

Isaiah 53 does not require a great deal of interpretation. The portrait is painted clearly enough for those with eyes to see:

> He was despised and forsaken of men, a man of sorrows and acquainted with grief; and like one from whom men hide their face, He was despised, and we did not esteem Him. Surely our griefs He Himself bore, and our sorrows He carried; yet we ourselves esteemed Him stricken, smitten of God, and afflicted. But He was pierced through for our transgressions, He was crushed for our iniquities; the chastening for our well-being fell upon Him, and by His scourging we are healed. All of us like sheep have gone astray, each of us has turned to his own way; but the Lord has caused the iniquity of us all to fall on Him. . . .
>
> He poured out Himself to death, and was numbered with the transgressors, yet He Himself bore the sin of many, and interceded for the transgressors.
>
> ISAIAH 53:3–6, 12

The present day rabbinic point of view concerning the Suffering Servant of this passage is that it describes Israel. This interpretation was first suggested around 1100 C.E. by the great rabbi Rashi in the midst of much persecution. The more the Christians tried to present Isaiah 53 as pertaining to Jesus, the more Rashi wanted to reinterpret it so it was no longer Messianic. By the 1500s it was an established interpretation.

While it is certainly true that the Jewish people have suffered greater atrocities than perhaps any other single group on the face of the earth, still Isaiah 53 is clearly *not* talking about Israel. It can't be. Try substituting *Israel* each time the prophet speaks of the "Servant" or "He" or "Him." It simply won't work. The plain sense of the text does not lend itself to support that modern Jewish interpretation of the passage. It has to be talking about a person.

When Philip (the evangelist) was traveling from Jerusalem to Gaza along an old desert road, he met an Ethiopian eunuch, most likely a proselyte to Judaism (Acts 8:26–40).

The eunuch "had come to Jerusalem to worship" and was sitting in his carriage, reading the prophet Isaiah. The Spirit of God told Philip, "Go up and join this carriage." It just so happened (a holy coincidence?) that the eunuch was reading Isaiah 53. Puzzled, he asked Philip, a Jewish believer in Jesus, "Please tell me, of whom does the prophet say this? Of himself, or of someone else?"

Philip got a chance to share about Jesus with his "neighbor." The eunuch was so excited to find the Messiah, he was ready to show his commitment by being baptized. This was not an unusual reponse for a Jewish believer, having its roots in the Jewish washing ceremonies and the teachings of John, the "immerser."

Without a doubt, Isaiah 53 is the most compelling of all the Messianic prophecies, describing the mission of the coming Messiah. What makes this prophecy particularly powerful is that Isaiah wrote it some 700 years before the coming of Messiah Jesus. That's what convinces us that God was involved in giving us this prophetic word.

Recently I shared this portion of Scripture with a member of my family. I didn't say anything about whom I thought it referred to. After reading the portion, my Jewish relative said, "But this doesn't say the Jews killed Jesus, does it?" She knew it referred to Jesus' death and apparently was still struggling with the anti-Semitic slur that the Jews killed Christ.

When I told her it certainly did not say that the Jews killed Jesus, but rather indicated that God was pleased with the sacrifice of the Suffering Servant, she felt better. Imagine her surprise when I pointed out that it was written 700 years before Jesus was born. Before we departed she asked, "Where was that portion of Scripture again?"

Isaiah is not the only prophet to describe the work of the Messiah. While he does give the clearest account of the substitutionary role—that of "Messiah, son of Joseph"—the role of the reigning King, "Messiah, son of David," is vividly portrayed for us by the prophet Zechariah.

## Zechariah 12–14: The Conquering King

Never before in the history of the world has the prophecy of Zechariah been more timely. Today we find Israel gathered in her own land, surrounded by hostile nations, outnumbered 100 to 1, unpopular with much of the rest of the world. One can almost see Zechariah's prophecy coming to pass, as if we are "in that day."

The setting for the prophecy is a day of danger for Israel. The beginnings of both chapter 12 and chapter 14 describe a time of enormous peril, with all the nations of the world gathered together to destroy Jerusalem. But in that day, God has promised to save His people.

The Lord warns that anyone who attacks Jerusalem will be severely hurt, for she will be a heavy stone to lift (12:3). Imagine the strain felt by someone who attempts to lift a weight heavier than he is able to bear. You can hear the anguish and see the grimace etched upon his face. You can feel the muscles of his back strain to the limit as the burden proves to be too much. Picturing this, we can understand the pain and frustration the hostile nations will suffer as they try in vain to budge God's fortress, Jerusalem.

Then, when the attack against Israel is at its worst, and it is apparent that no other nation can or will help Israel, even if some nations who would like to will not be able to, Israel will call upon God for help. God will then pour out His Spirit upon the house of David and the inhabitants of Jerusalem, giving "the spirit of grace and of supplication." This outpouring will cause the Jewish people to "look on Me whom they have pierced; and . . . mourn for Him, as one mourns for an only son" (Zechariah 12:10). No one can recognize the truth of the Messiah unless it is revealed by the Spirit of God. Here, "in that day," when the Spirit is poured out, all of Israel will have open eyes, eyes to know their Messiah.

In that day, when all the nations gather themselves against Jerusalem, God Himself will go forth and fight on behalf of His people. His feet will stand on the Mount of Olives (Zechariah 14:4) and He will rebuff those who have dared to attack God's chosen people. The Mount of Olives is the site where Jesus wept over Jerusalem, lamenting the suffering His people would undergo because of their refusal to accept Him (Matthew 23:37). It is the place from where Jesus ascended into heaven (Luke 24:50). It is the place where He shall return (Zechariah 14:4).

Zechariah 13:1 promises a fountain, open to the house of David and for the inhabitants of Jerusalem, to provide cleansing of sin and impurity. In that day cleansing for Israel will be found in the sacrifice of the Messiah.

In that day living water will flow from Jerusalem (Zechariah 14:8). The promise of spiritual life will issue from the heart of God. Jesus talking to the woman at the well informed her that He was the Source of that living water (John 4:14).

Finally, those nations that remain following the attack on Israel (these will be individuals who have sided with God) will go to Jerusalem year after year to worship the King, the Lord of hosts. Complete now will be the Messiah's final mission; accomplished will be His ultimate goal—to reign as King over all the earth.

Obviously, these prophecies in Zechariah have not yet been fulfilled. All the nations of the world have not yet turned against Israel. The Spirit has not yet been poured out upon the Jewish people. The Lord has not yet returned to the Mount of Olives. This will yet be fulfilled at the second appearing of the Messiah.

Thus, the two purposes of the Messiah are clearly outlined in these two Messianic prophecies. The first purpose, that of Suffering Servant—Messiah, son of Joseph—is depicted in Isaiah 53. The second purpose, that of conquering king—Messiah, son of David—is described in Zechariah 12–14. These two passages of Messianic prophecy can be powerfully presented to persuade Jewish people that Jesus is the Messiah. And there are many more that support this.

### Zechariah 9:9: The Entering King

Zechariah 9:9 tells us by what means of transportation the Messiah would come to Jerusalem. He would ride on a young donkey. This certainly has a peculiar ring, and it paints for us a curious picture. One might think that the Messiah would enter the city where He would one day reign riding a formidable white steed, an entrance not at all uncommon in the days of Jesus.

Ordinarily, a king would enter a city sitting grandly astride a war horse, both horse and rider armored for battle. This exhibit of strength and power was designed to intimidate his foes. We see this done today when various nations participate in military exercises to show others their might.

The Messiah would come on a young donkey because His was a mission of peace, not military conquest. Matthew 21:2–6 describes the fulfillment of this prophecy as Jesus rode into Jerusalem on a donkey in "triumphal entry." His was a display of meekness, not of might.

### 2 Samuel 7:12–17: The Everlasting King

This portion of Scripture accomplished two things at once. It prophesied that a son of King David would reign over Israel, and that the Kingdom under David's throne would endure forever.

David's life was drawing to its close. God had sent Nathan the prophet to the king to offer him a promise of hope in his declining years. Speaking of Solomon, Nathan said:

> "When your days are complete and you lie down with your fathers,
> I will raise up your descendant after you, who will come forth from
> you, and I will establish his kingdom. He shall build a house for
> My name."

Then the prophet says something unusual:

> "And I will establish the throne of his kingdom forever."
>
> 2 SAMUEL 7:12–13

Solomon did indeed "build a house for My [God's] name." But Solomon did not live or rule forever. How, then, was the throne of his kingdom to continue eternally, especially given the fact that Solomon's Temple was eventually destroyed and that Israel no longer crowns kings? The answer is through the Messiah. This Son, or descendant of David, would ultimately establish an everlasting Kingdom.

In studying the genealogies of Jesus we find that He was, in fact, a descendant of David. The first chapter of Matthew traces Jesus' heritage from Abraham, to David, to Joseph, his adoptive father, emphasizing that Jesus was legal heir to the promises given Abraham and David. Luke 3 gives Mary's line, showing Jesus' blood descent from David. Mary's—or to use her Jewish name, Miriam's—genealogy, in accord with Jewish usage, is given in her husband's name. That is, Joseph was the son-in-law of Eli.

Furthermore, after Jesus' death and ascension into heaven He took "His seat at the right hand of the throne of the Majesty in the heavens" (Hebrews 8:1). In Revelation 1:5 John declares Him to be "ruler of the kings of the earth."

Jesus was truly a son of David, and He reigns eternally.

### Isaiah 7:14: The Miraculous Birth of the Messiah

Most believers know the verse so often quoted at Christmas, "Behold, a virgin shall be with child, and shall bring forth a son, and they shall call his name Emmanuel, which being interpreted is, God with us" (Matthew 1:23, KJV). Matthew, writing by the inspiration of the Holy Spirit, considers this prophecy, given to Isaiah, to have found its fulfillment in the miraculous birth of Jesus. This is a powerful prophecy in that it is so specific.

You need to be aware, however, that you may get some argument from your Jewish friend about the use of the words *ha alma*, the words translated in Isaiah as "the virgin." Technically, *alma* means "young woman"; there is another Hebrew word that specifically means "virgin."

Isaiah 7:14 is a valid and usable Messianic prophecy, but unless you engage in detailed study of the nature of this verse, perhaps it might not be the best one for you to present.

It might help to point out that God used miraculous births in the creation of the Jewish people, so it shouldn't surprise us that He used a miraculous birth to save His people, too. The "birth" of Adam and Eve was a miracle. The wives of Abraham, Isaac, and Jacob were all barren until God opened their wombs to give life to the children of Israel. So it can be argued that God, bringing the Messiah through a miraculous birth, is perfectly consistent with the way the Almighty worked in times past.

### Isaiah 9:6: Messiah's Incredible Name

The verse we just discussed, Isaiah 7:14, is found in a section that has been referred to as the "Book of Emmanuel." This rich portion of the book of Isaiah includes another great Messianic prophecy, Isaiah 9:6:

> For a child will be born to us, a son will be given to us; and the government will rest on His shoulders; and His name will be called Wonderful Counselor, Mighty God, Eternal Father, Prince of Peace.

This phenomenal prophecy describes the Messianic reign and attributes of the little Baby who was later born in Bethlehem. No Jew in history could be described with these names, no Jew except Jesus.

### Jeremiah 31:31–33: A New Covenant

Jewish people might challenge you about the New Testament: "Where were we told that we needed another Testament? Isn't one enough?"

The answer to this question can be found in Jeremiah 31:31–33. Through Jeremiah, God promised a new covenant to His people, different from the former covenant, the Mosaic covenant. Under the new covenant God promised to write His Law on the hearts of His people instead of just writing it on tablets of stone.

During His final Passover with His disciples, Jesus referred to the cup of wine He handed them to drink as the "new covenant" in His blood (Luke 22:20). When a person becomes a believer in Jesus and receives God's Spirit, there is a new law written on his heart, one that offers forgiveness for sin because of Jesus' perfect sacrifice.

This is not to imply that it's wrong to keep the commandments, even the very letter of the Law. The Law that God gave, extolled at great length in Psalm 119, is holy, righteous, and good. If, however, the Law is kept *only* externally, with a heart far from God, then observing the Law is an empty exercise.

Having a faith relationship with God is the most important aspect of the spiritual life. Because of that relationship, a person will be committed to performing godly deeds. Following God's ways is a consequence *of* salvation, not a condition *for* salvation.

Jeremiah promised that a new covenant would someday shift the observance of God's Law from an external exercise to an internal instinct.

### Daniel 9:24–27: When Would the Messiah Come?

Soon after I was first confronted with the message of the Messiah I struggled with a dilemma. I found myself beginning to believe the

Gospel. This frightened me, because I knew if I professed belief in Jesus, it would change the course of the rest of my life.

I was still studying and practicing transcendental meditation, still expecting to become a teacher of this technique. Suddenly Jesus entered the picture. If He was really the Messiah, I'd have to regroup, retrain, and redirect my life. It was a terrifying thought.

On top of this, I already suspected that although my parents and friends might not disown me, they certainly would dissociate from me. To some extent this happened. (This is not unusual for Jewish believers, but you should know that relationships with my family, after going through some upheaval, have become better than ever. I tell you this so you might help your Jewish neighbor deal with possible fears.)

It was Thursday, the night of Dan Rigney's Bible study. Instead of continuing in Isaiah, we turned to Daniel. I felt a bit relieved, thinking that I was finally on familiar ground. Daniel, after all, was the one from the lion's den and the fiery furnace, the Daniel I had learned about when I was a child. I didn't know anything about Isaiah.

What I didn't know was that God had revealed to Daniel the precise timing of the coming of His Messiah. *Wow,* I thought as we entered into a study of Daniel 9. *This will really clinch it for me.* Verse 24 talked about a certain amount of time, after which the Messiah would come, transgression would be finished, iniquity atoned for, everlasting righteousness brought in, and an anointing (that's like saying a "Messiah-ing") of the most holy place.

Verse 26 knocked me over. It said that in connection with this period the Messiah would be cut off—killed. Then, after the Messiah's death, the city (Jerusalem) and the sanctuary (the Temple) would be destroyed. Both Jerusalem and the Temple had been destroyed in 70 C.E.! That meant the Messiah had to have died *before* 70 C.E.

Daniel 9 immediately brought me one step closer to making a decision to believe. But something else hit me at exactly the same time. If all this was as clear as it seemed to me that day, then why didn't the rabbis see it? I figured that I'd better get myself over to a rabbi before I fell for something that wasn't true. I realized that either my fellow Jews had, for the most part, missed the Messiah, or all my Christian friends were submitting to a lie. I had to know.

Since I did not know any rabbis personally, I trekked over to my folks' house to find out if they did. My dad referred me to a rabbi in downtown Washington, D.C. I set up an appointment to talk with him. Bringing a Bible into his office I asked, "Rabbi, would you please explain to me the 'Jewish' interpretation of Daniel chapter 9?"

His response jolted me. "I advise you," he said, "not to study the Bible. When you do you get all confused."

"But Rabbi," I protested, "don't you believe in God?"

I will always remember his response. "God," he mused, "is a good hypothesis!"

I was shocked. When I left his office I was so disoriented I couldn't even find my car. I knew what I needed—to find a rabbi who truly believed in God and accepted the Bible as His Word. But I didn't know any Orthodox rabbis whom I could contact.

When I went to work the next day, a strange "coincidence" occurred. The front door opened and in walked a man I had never seen before. He had a long white beard, and the dark clothing that identified him as an Orthodox rabbi. I just about jumped on him.

"Rabbi, I must study with you!" I cried.

"Do you want to be a rabbi?" he asked.

I shook my head. "I don't know, I just want to know the truth."

The kind rabbi invited me to his home to study with him, and I did so for several weeks. When I asked him about Daniel 9 he simply said that he was not allowed to study that portion of Scripture, for it calculated the time of the coming of Messiah.

"So," I said, "why can't you study that?"

He looked solemn. "The Talmud forbids us to calculate the coming of the Messiah." This, he explained, was to prevent speculation and possible loss of faith should the Messiah not come at the calculated time.

Now I was convinced. If the old rabbi was right—that Daniel foretold the coming of the Messiah—and if the calculations I had *already* made were correct, Jesus *had* to be the Messiah.

In witnessing to your Jewish neighbor, it is not always necessary to go into great detail concerning these calculations. Often it is enough to show that there is a time period that concludes with the death of the Messiah (for the purpose of putting an end to iniquity) and that this time period is to be completed before the destruction of the Temple in 70 C.E..

Daniel 9, like Isaiah 53, is one of the most powerful of the Messianic prophecies.

### Micah 5:2: The Birthplace of Messiah

Not only did God reveal *why, how,* and *when* the Messiah would come, He also was specific about *where* He would be born. Micah 5:2 reads:

> "But as for you, Bethlehem Ephrathah, too little to be among the clans of Judah, from you One will go forth for Me to be ruler in Israel. His goings forth are from long ago, from the days of eternity."

God chose a humble town for Messiah's birth, Bethlehem, the city of David, the birthplace of Jesus.

Matthew refers to this verse in chaper 2 of his Gospel. When Herod gathered the chief priests and scribes together and asked them where the Messiah was to be born, they quoted Micah 5:2. This prophecy was clearly considered Messianic in the days of Jesus.

## Presenting Messianic Prophecy

Now that you are armed with prophecies for presenting the Messiah to your Jewish neighbor, let me caution you. It is very important to be humble, yet firm, in your discussion of these prophetic passages. It is new and unfamiliar ground for most Jewish people. Further, there has been some valid criticism concerning the way these verses are sometimes used and interpreted.

Believers are accused of lifting verses of Scripture out of their historical context. To some extent that is true. It isn't that those portions are not Messianic prophecies. They are. But *how* they are Messianic is not always understood, and the settings in which God gave them can also be wrongly ignored.

Nevertheless, do not hesitate to present Messianic prophecy in your effort to share the Gospel. Messianic prophecies are part of the Word of God and were given to help His people find His Messiah. Many testimonies of Jewish believers include reference to the passages we have looked at here.

# 7

# Semantics and Sensitivities
## —or—
### *How to Build Bridges . . . Not Walls*

I stood in front of a sea of blank faces. It was taking me awhile to get the point across to my general semantics class at Howard University where I was teaching.

"The word is not the thing," I repeated once again. But somehow this basic principle of semantics was not hitting home. "For instance," I continued, "the word *dog* is not the dog itself. It is only a sound that stands for the animal—a symbol; the dog itself is called the referent."

I then asked everyone in the class to draw a picture illustrating the word *dog*. Soon there were pictures of huge dogs and tiny ones. There were black dogs, red dogs, white dogs; mean-looking dogs, wimpy little dogs. Someone even drew a hot dog. The exercise finally got the point across. Words can sometimes be a poor form of communication, but they are the tools that we have to work with.

It's important to understand that whereas a word may mean one thing to you it will often convey a different meaning to someone else. In talking to your Jewish neighbor about Jesus, this principle is especially operative. Let us spend a moment to consider the difference between "denotative" and "connotative" meanings.

The denotative meaning of a word is its original technical meaning. For example, the word *water*, denotatively, is "$H_2O$." Water is composed of two atoms of hydrogen and one atom of oxygen. That's its denotative meaning.

Connotatively, however, *water* means so much more. It might connote a summer's vacation at the beach. It might call forth the frustration of bailing out a flooded basement. It might evoke the memory of guzzling a big glass of it after mowing the lawn.

Thus, the word *water* carries both denotative and connotative meanings. The word *water* is not the thing itself. This is the nature of semantics. *The word is not the thing, it is a symbol that stands for the thing.* Nowhere is this seen more clearly than in sharing the message of the Messiah with your Jewish neighbor.

The fellow in my Coast Guard Reserve unit witnessed to me using semantically sensitive language. His choice of words arrested my attention and got me to consider the claims of Jesus. As I mentioned earlier, in answer to my question about that elusive peace he seemed to have, he smiled and said, "Your Messiah lives in my heart."

He used the term *Messiah*, derived from the Hebrew *Mashiach*, meaning "anointed one." In Greek, the word for *anointed* is *Christos*, commonly "Christ." *Messiah* and *Christ* mean exactly the same thing technically, or denotatively. They can both be defined by the single English word *anointed*. But connotatively, they convey two entirely different meanings. Here is a classic case where the word is definitely not the thing.

To a Jewish person, Christ is the last name of the Gentile deity. I was surprised at how many non-Jewish Christians think that, too. To a Jewish person, Christ conducted the Crusades, invoked the Inquisition, and prompted the persecution of Jews over the last twenty centuries. To a Jewish person, Christ is the first part of the term used by those who use the accusation of deicide: "Christ-killers!"

If that fellow in the Coast Guard had told me that "Christ lived in his heart," it would have meant something entirely different to me. I would have thought to myself, *Well, that's nice for you. You're supposed to believe that stuff. But it's got nothing to do with me. Maybe I should consider how to have more of Moses in my heart.* His whole point would have been lost because he did not use semantically sensitive language.

Connotatively, *Christ* does not equal *Messiah* in the mind of a Jewish person. Jewish people are more comfortable with the term *Messiah*, even though most Jews don't embrace a Messianic hope. (More on that in Section III.)

So if you are talking about the anointed One, the Christ, why not say it the Jewish way—Messiah! It makes for more effective communication.

Christians use other semantically "loaded" terms in witnessing. Some terminology can be replaced with language that is less offensive, less ambiguous, and still makes the same point, only better. The apostle Paul advised the Corinthian believers, "Give no offense either to Jews or to Greeks or to the church of God" (1 Corinthians 10:32). Even though he was writing to a Gentile church, he was nevertheless quick to advise them not to offend Jews and others in their witness.

All groups develop a particular jargon, a unique way of saying something. Those who conform to the ways the group uses the jargon are considered the "in group." Those who don't are considered "out." It is certainly not your goal to shut the door on your Jewish neighbor, making him or her feel excluded from the family of God. Instead, you want to use language to draw the person in, to communicate, truly communicate, all that God has offered in Jesus. Words are tools that God has given us for communication. How much more effective we can be with skilled use of this precious tool!

I urge you to consider learning and using those words that are less offensive to Jews and that, at the same time, clearly communicate biblical truth. You will not just become a better communicator; you will also gain a new perspective on many of the doctrines of the faith.

The following list contains words that can be either confusing or objectionable to Jewish people. I have also attempted to explain the reason for suggesting a change.

## Semantic Substitutes for a Sensitive Witness

1. Instead of using the description *Christian,* say *Messianic, biblical,* or *scriptural.*

To a Jewish person, the adjective *Christian* does not describe a follower of the Messiah of Israel. It means someone who is a non-Jewish churchgoer, Catholic, Episcopalian, Baptist, Presbyterian, etc. It makes little difference if the person is "born again" or is even practicing the Christian faith. Being Jewish is a matter of birth. Therefore, being Christian is also seen as a matter of birth.

*Messianic* or *biblical* has the same meaning and communicates something Jewish.

*EXAMPLE:* "That was not a very biblical thing to do," instead of, "That was not a Christian thing to do." Or, "We follow the Messianic faith," rather than, "We are Christians."

**2. Instead of calling someone a *Christian* try the term *believer*.**

*Christian* means "one who follows Christ." To a Jew, *Christian* is equated with *Gentile* and has little to do with the Messiah or anything Jewish. That's why *believer* or *believer in Jesus* is more communicative.

*EXAMPLE:* "I am a believer in the Messiah," instead of, "I am a Christian."

**3. Instead of using the Greek word *Christ,* use the term *Messiah*.**

As explained already, *Christ* is not understood to mean "anointed one"; it is presumed, instead, to be the last name of the Gentile deity. *Messiah* is a more familiar word to represent the same Person.

*EXAMPLE:* "I follow Jesus, the Messiah," instead of, "Jesus Christ is my Lord."

**4. Instead of referring to your place of worship as a *church,* call it a *congregation*.**

Although *church* means "called-out body of believers"—Jews *and* Gentiles—to a Jew, church is the place Gentiles go to worship on Sunday. It is not something with which Jews are traditionally involved. A word that can be substituted is *congregation* since that is what most Jewish people call their place of worship.

*EXAMPLE:* "I just came back from services in my congregation," instead of, "I just came back from church."

**5. Instead of using the Greek name *Jesus,* try calling Him by the name He was called by His family and disciples, *Yeshua* (short for Yehoshua, or Joshua).**

Many Jewish people have a hard time saying the name *Jesus.* Many were taught never to utter His name in their homes. Since His followers called Him *Yeshua,* His Hebrew name, rather than *Jesus,* the Greek rendering of His name, it is acceptable to use His Hebrew name. Both names, one Greek, one Hebrew, denote the same meaning—Savior. But connotatively, one is Jewish while the other is quite Gentile.

*EXAMPLE:* "Joseph and Miriam had a son named Yeshua."

**6. Instead of saying that Jesus *died for my sins,* try using the phrase *atoned for my sins.***

The word *atonement* is more familiar to Jewish people since the Day of Atonement is observed each year. Jesus' sacrifice was the fulfillment of this holy day. It's clearer if you relate that fact in your witness.

*EXAMPLE:* "Messiah Yeshua atoned for my sins," instead of, "Christ died for my sins."

**7. Instead of referring to the Comforter as the *Holy Spirit* or *Holy Ghost,* it might be better to speak of Him as the *Spirit of God.***

Although the title *Holy Spirit* does appear in the Old Testament (*Holy Ghost* in the King James Version), it rings of Roman Catholicism in a Jewish ear. It also emphasizes the concept of the Trinity, a difficult idea for even Christians to comprehend. *Spirit of God* is a term found in Genesis 1:2.

*EXAMPLE:* "He is filled with the Spirit of God," instead of, "He is filled with the Holy Ghost."

**8. Instead of using the word *Trinity,* a different emphasis can be brought out by using the term *composite unity.***

The term *Trinity* is not found in Scripture. It is a manmade attempt developed at the Council of Nicea to describe the mysterious and unique nature of God. At first hearing, it sounds polytheistic, not monotheistic. Since the central tenet of faith for Jews is the belief in one God, the use of *Trinity* could confuse the issue. (See Section IV.)

*EXAMPLE:* "We believe in the composite unity of God," instead of, "We believe in the Trinity."

**9. Instead of calling the salvation message the *Gospel,* speak of it as the *Good News.***

To a Jew, the message of the Gospel has seemed like bad news, not good news. Those bearing the message have often persecuted Jews. It's good to define the word, since the term *Gospel* has only negative connotations.

*EXAMPLE:* "I am sharing the Good News that the Messiah came to atone for sin," instead of, "I am a minister of the Gospel of Jesus Christ."

**10. Instead of celebrating *Easter,* emphasize the fact that it's *Resurrection Day.***

Easter connotes eggs, bonnets, parades, *and* anti-Semitism. As we have already mentioned, the name is derived from that of the pagan goddess Ishtar, and was picked up by the Church centuries ago. It has little to do with the concept of resurrection, which, as we will see in Section IV, *is* Jewish.

*EXAMPLE:* "We are attending our Resurrection Day services," instead of, "We are going to Easter services."

**11. Instead of using the word *Christmas,* why not call it the *Messiah's birthday?***

Again, the word *Christmas* is associated with more than just the birth of the Messiah. It connotes tinsel, trees, Santa Claus. These are all pleasant traditions for Gentiles. They do not have much relevance for Jews. But the birth of Messiah is of critical importance to Jewish people, or at least should be.

*EXAMPLE:* "We celebrate Messiah's birthday," instead of "Merry Christmas."

**12. Instead of *Pentecost,* refer to the holiday as *Shavuot.***

The holiday discussed in Acts 2 was the biblical holiday known as Shavuot (pronounced "*Shah*-voo-oat"). Pentecost is the Greek way of saying it. To Jewish people, when they hear about Pentecost, all they can think about is Pentecostalism and the extremes associated with that movement—snake-handling and rolling in the aisles—something to which most Jews can't relate. But Pentecost was the Jewish holiday known as Shavuot.

*EXAMPLE:* "The believers were gathered for Shavuot," instead of, "The Christians were gathered for Pentecost."

**13. Instead of looking forward to the *Second Coming of Christ,* how about anticipating the *return of the Messiah?***

Think how much more is communicated to Jewish people when you say, "I look forward to the return of the Messiah," rather than, "I am awaiting the Second Coming of Christ."

**14. Instead of calling the second portion of the holy Scriptures the *New Testament,* another way to refer to it is the *New Covenant* or *Br'it Chadashah.***

As you learned from the section on Messianic prophecy, God promised the Jewish people that He would make with them a "new covenant." This term, in either English or Hebrew (pronounced "Brit Hah-dah-*shah*") will feel more relevant to your Jewish neighbor. The New Testament is seen as the Gentile Bible.

*EXAMPLE:* "This is found in the New Covenant, or *Br'it Chadashah,*" instead of "the New Testament."

**15. Instead of calling the first part of the Bible the *Old Testament,* try saying, *Tenakh* or *Hebrew Scripture.***

To a Jew, the portion of the Bible with which he is familiar is not old. It is relevant today. In a way, it is offensive to call someone's guidebook "old." Tenakh includes Torah (the five books of Moses), Neviim (the prophets), and Ketuvim (the writings). This T-N-K acronym is how Jewish people refer to the Bible. Sometimes, it is called Torah, expanding the term beyond the five books of Moses.

*EXAMPLE:* "We are studying Tenakh," rather than, "We are studying the Old Testament."

16. **Instead of saying** *baptism,* **say** *immersion* **or** *mikveh* (**the ritual purification through bathing**).

There are, of course, widely varying opinions among believers as to the prescribed mode of baptism. Nevertheless, for the sake of your Jewish friend or neighbor who cares little for the controversy but for whom the word *baptize* carries unpleasant connotations, why not substitute the word *immerse?* Regardless of your personal feelings about the preferred mode of baptism, it will represent a better point of identification with him.

If you will recall what I shared with you about the Jews during the Spanish Inquisition, you will understand why *baptism* is a sensitive word today. In Spain, Jews were forced to be baptized. It wasn't in response to true faith; it was the result of forced compliance. The true origin of the act of baptizing goes back to the Jewish traditions associated with symbolic cleansing, today called *mikveh.* John the "Immerser" put his followers through this ceremony so they could symbolize their identification with his message and show their internal conviction to turn from sin. In like manner, being immersed in the name of Yeshua means identifying with His message.

*EXAMPLE:* Instead of saying, "I've been baptized in the name of the Father, Son, and Holy Ghost," say, "I've been immersed showing my identification with the God of Abraham, Isaac, and Jacob, His Spirit, and Yeshua, the Messiah." I know that's a little *klutzy* (awkward), but you get the point.

17. **Instead of saying** *cross,* **say** *tree* **or** *altar* **or even** *execution stake.*

Although the cross represents the culmination of Yeshua's earthly ministry, people have ruined the real meaning of love that was demonstrated there. Instead of seeing the cross as the site of salvation, Jews now view it as a place of persecution. As we saw earlier, the cross is regarded with fear by Jewish people.

18. **Instead of using the word** *conversion,* **say** *turning* **or** *completion* **depending on the context.**

The Bible uses the term *conversion* to mean turning away from sin and toward God. But in our society, *conversion* has come to mean the changing of religions. When a Jew accepts Yeshua, he does turn from sin and toward God, but he does not change religions. He is receiving the salvation promised in Tenakh.

*EXAMPLE*: Instead of saying, "converted Jew," say "completed Jew" or "Messianic Jew" (or Gentile).

This list is by no means exhaustive. But it offers you the prime examples of words and phrases that can be modified to bring the Gospel message closer to the heart of your Jewish neighbor. By making these small adjustments in speech, you will not only be taking into account the connotative meanings of these emotionally charged words, but you will also gain further insight into the Jewish roots of your own faith.

Now that you are familiar with "Messianic terminology," why don't we put into practice what you've just learned? We will use "Messianic terminology" throughout the rest of the book. It will give you an opportunity to feel more comfortable using this sensitized language.

# SECTION III

## The Audience: Your Jewish Neighbor

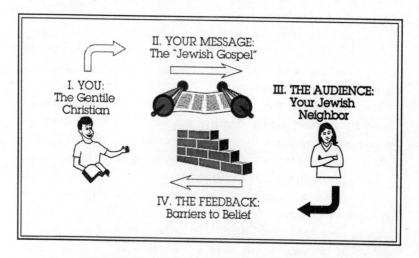

I. YOU:
The Gentile Christian

II. YOUR MESSAGE:
The "Jewish Gospel"

III. THE AUDIENCE:
Your Jewish Neighbor

IV. THE FEEDBACK:
Barriers to Belief

A Jewish-believer friend of mine used to sell jewelry. Once, when we were discussing ways to communicate the message of the Messiah more effectively, she said that in sales the words she lived by were *Know your customer!* I can affirm that this is true because of a recent transaction I had with a car salesman.

It was time for us to buy a new car. Steffi was still driving the Volvo we had purchased right after getting married in 1975. Although the car is still doing fine (I drive it now), she needed something more suited to her life as a suburbanite with two children who have lots of friends.,

We decided to check out the new mini-vans and headed for our nearest dealer. Four years earlier, I had purchased a car at that very place, the car we were now trading in on the van. I still remembered the salesman who had persuaded me to spend thousands of dollars on that little car. He was an m.o.t., a member of the tribe. In other words, he was Jewish.

An unusual thing about this particular dealership is that it is owned and run predominantly by Arabs. But they have a few Jewish salesmen and it was one of these who had helped me purchase the car. This same salesman approached us now as we returned to buy the van.

I was impressed that he remembered my name. "Mr. and Mrs. Rubin, how nice to see you again! How are your two lovely daughters?" I liked him. Right away, I was ready to buy!

The man had taken pains to "know his customer."

This is a basic principle of all good communication. In classes on public speaking and persuasion, the importance of "audience analysis" is always stressed.

Few examples of this stand out more than John F. Kennedy's *Ich bin ein Berliner* speech. Sensing the need to identify with his German audience, Kennedy spoke in German, referring to himself as their fellow countryman. As a result, he brought the house down. He knew his audience and identified with them. They loved him.

This section will introduce you to your Jewish neighbors. You may know their names. You may know the names of their children. You may even have established a comfortable relationship, sharing some of the intimate details of your lives. But there's always room to learn more, right?

I hope these chapters help dispel some common misconceptions you might have about the Jewish people, and help you better understand Jewish history, religion, culture, and values.

So here goes. Let me introduce you to your Jewish neighbor!

# 8

# Misconceptions About Jewish People
## —or—
## *All Jews Aren't Created Equal*

It's easy to draw erroneous conclusions about a person you barely know. These conclusions, or stereotypes, often reveal prejudice. How many times we wrongly prejudge another, sometimes leading to harmful consequences.

Stereotypes can easily become etched into one's mind. Stereotypes about blacks. About women. About the elderly. About children. Stereotypes cause serious problems in our society.

Stereotypes about Jews present yet another unique problem. They have precipitated a situation that has seriously hampered the spread of the Gospel among God's chosen people.

In this chapter I hope to dispel some of these misconceptions, these stereotypes, in an attempt to enhance your understanding of your Jewish neighbor. To make it easier, these misconceptions will be divided into two sections—personal and spiritual.

## Personal Misconceptions

Asked to describe the physical characteristics of a Jew, it would not be surprising to hear references to a large nose, short stature, and curly black hair. Where these stereotypes originated exactly, I do not know. The truth is that not all Jews have big noses. Not all Jews are short. Not all Jews have curly black hair. Stereotypes are just not always true.

Asked to describe the behavioral characteristics of the Jewish people, the words *stingy* or *bookish* might come to mind. Perhaps it was Shakespeare's Shylock or Dickens' Fagin that gave rise to the "stingy" myth. It is true that one Jew, Jack Benny, deliberately exaggerated this stereotype. But if Mr. Benny's true generosity had become known, it would have destroyed his public image as a tightwad. Jews are no stingier than other people. Indeed, many Jewish people are downright philanthropic.

The stereotype of the Jewish intellectual may stem from the many Jews who have made contributions to the fields of art and science. As a general rule, education is emphasized in the homes of

Jewish families, although the same can be said of other groups as well. In addition, of course, not all Jews are that educated.

The source of these stereotypes is not really that important for our purposes. What remains for us is to understand that stereotypes and misconceptions will not help you know your Jewish neighbor, and may actually hinder your ability to communicate the Gospel to him or her.

This is probably not a revelation to you. Anyone interested enough in the Jewish people to get this book would likely add a resounding "amen" to these thoughts. And though you may not indulge in "Jewish" jokes or revert to habits of personal stereotyping, there often remain, even among believers, certain misconceptions about the Jewish people. These usually surface when it comes to the discussion of spiritual subjects.

## Spiritual Stereotypes

Not long ago, while I was conducting a seminar on sharing the Messiah with Jewish people, I was asked a question by one of the church members: "What do Jews think the Messiah will be like?" It seemed a logical question raised by a believer who wanted to better understand his Jewish neighbor. My answer shocked the audience.

I explained that most Jews don't believe in the coming of a personal Messiah. The participants could hardly believe their ears. Certainly, they supposed, the people to whom the Messiah was promised would be awaiting His appearance.

Sadly, today's Jewish person has little or no concern with the coming of a personal Messiah. After the Holocaust, many Jews lost hope. Certainly there are some who still do believe, but for those Jews who denied a personal Messiah, but still wanted to hold some hope, a "Messianic age" concept developed. Their belief is the hope that humankind will "evolve" into a higher state of consciousness. That was the view I held when I jumped into transcendental meditation.

The misconception that Jews believe in the coming Messiah has led to some real problems in the witness of many believers. Believing that all it will take are a few rightly applied Messianic prophecies, a believer may find himself up against an unexpected shrug of apathy. The fact is, your Jewish neighbor is not sitting around waiting for the Messiah—wondering where He would be born, who His ancestors were, or what His ministry would accomplish.

Many believers, therefore, find themselves answering questions their Jewish neighbors have never even thought of, much less asked. It takes awhile to earn enough trust to talk about personal things like a relationship with God. You can't just jump into Messianic prophecy. The conclusion of this book, "Putting It All Together," will talk about this in greater detail. For now, though, you need to understand that although you may be absolutely clear on how to show that Messiah is shown in the Tenakh, your Jewish friend might simply say, "Well, I don't believe in the Messiah, anyway."

Perhaps you've always assumed that all Jewish people share the same theology. Nothing could be further from the truth. Along with varying degrees of Bible knowledge and differing Messianic expectations, you will find that Jewish people hold extremely diverse opinions about God, the afterlife, Israel, and most other subjects.

These next chapters should help you get to know your Jewish neighbor in the areas of history, religion, and culture. They are designed to provide you with an overview and will, therefore, be general. Certainly not all of the information will apply to *your* Jewish neighbor. Remember all we said about stereotyping and misconceptions. So, forewarned and forearmed, let's take a look at the history of the Jewish people.

# 9

# A Brief History of the Jewish People
## —*or*—
## *The Wanderings of the Wandering Jews*

$T_o$ condense 4,000 years of history into a few pages is an impossible task. This would be true even if the people we were considering led routine lives. But Jews! A community that has heard the voice of God, a nation that has inhabited nearly the entire planet, a people from whom the Messiah came—no, condensing the history of the Jews is not easy. But some history is necessary to help you in your witness.

We'll begin with the assumption that you are pretty familiar with biblical Jewish history from years of sermons and Sunday school. So we will focus primarily on post-biblical times. A few key biblical events, however, should be laid out as a foundation for the rest.

## From Abraham to the Babylonian Captivity: The Beginnings of the Jewish Nation and the First Commonwealth

The Jewish people began when God called Abram out of Ur of the Chaldees. His willingness to respond to God's call was indicative of his great faith. God chose to bless Abram, changing his name to Abraham, "the father of a multitude," promising that his descendants would be as numerous as the stars in the heaven and the dust of the earth.

This people continued through Isaac, and Isaac's son Jacob. The nation grew in number when the Jews lived in Egypt where they eventually became slaves. God, however, remembering His covenant, planned to bring them to the land He had promised to the patriarchs. With Moses as deliverer, the people were led out of bondage and into freedom.

Through these first five books of the Bible, the Torah, Abraham, Isaac, Jacob, and Moses are the most prominent figures, and Jewish people tend to be most familiar with them. Abraham, Isaac, and Jacob are often mentioned in the prayers of Jewish people. For example, "God of Abraham, Isaac, and Jacob. . . ." This identifies

God, the same God you worship. You might even try using this expression when sharing with your Jewish friend.

Moses is affectionately called *Moshe Rabbenu*, "Moses our master or teacher." He is held in the highest esteem, not only as a great teacher of truth as evidenced in the Torah, but as the one who led the Jewish people out of bondage. On Passover, an annual celebration even the most secular Jews generally observe, Moses is mentioned over and over.

Referring to the patriarchs or Moses will place your Jewish neighbor on familiar territory, and the two of you on common ground.

After Moses died, Joshua (whose name, as we have seen, is the Hebrew equivalent of *Jesus*) led the people into the Promised Land. They entered with the Torah—the Law, the set of rules and regulations for life in the land God had given them. The people, having heard all that God required, had ratified the covenant, promising to do what the Lord had demanded.

Upon entering the Promised Land, Israel had to conquer the many nations living there. Joshua led the conquest and following his death Israel was ruled by the judges. All the while, the Jewish people encountered tremendous opposition to their right to live in the Promised Land.

Soon, the temptation to mix with the surrounding nations and to adopt some of their practices caused the Jews further problems. An example of this is seen in the way in which Israel was to be governed. Although it was clear that God wanted to remain the unique Ruler of Israel, the Jewish people, surrounded by earthly monarchies, demanded that God provide for them a human king.

The first king, Saul, turned out to be a disaster for the Jewish people. God had warned them this would happen. In His grace, as a replacement for Saul, He provided a decent—although not perfect—king for His people. That king was David. Through David, God revealed many truths to His people, some concerning David's future descendant, Yeshua. It was David whom the Lord used to bring forth many psalms that point to the Messiah—among them Psalm 2, Psalm 22, and Psalm 110. These can also be used as

Messianic prophecies, but because David is known as a poet, not a prophet, they might be more subject to question.

After the reign of David and his son Solomon came the period of the kings. The Jewish nation had become divided into the Northern Kingdom, known as Israel, and the Southern Kingdom, called Judah. Both kingdoms wandered into the ways of pagans in spite of the prophetic messages God sent them. Although the primary purpose of the prophets was to realign the people of Israel with God's original plan and purpose, the prophets also shared predictions from God, prophetic messages concerning the coming Messiah.

In 721 B.C.E. the Northern Kingdom was taken into captivity by Assyria as a punishment for walking in ways of ungodliness. In 586 B.C.E. the Southern Kingdom, too, was taken captive, this time by the Babylonians. The Jews were no longer in the Promised Land. It was during this period of captivity that God raised up certain prophets to give the people hope and guidance. Daniel, the one through whom God revealed the time of Messiah's coming, prophesied during this period.

## From the Babylonian Captivity to the Great Dispersion: The Second Commonwealth

The *sopherim*, the scribes, occupied high positions during the monarchical period. Later, without kings to assist, they were free to delve more deeply into the study of the Law of Moses and the writings of the Jewish people. Ezra was described as "scribe of the Law of the God of heaven," equivalent to our Secretary of Education. Just as the office of high priest replaced the office of king in Israeli government, so, too, did the office of scribe replace the office of prophet in religion. The influence of the scribes grew during the post-exilic period and through the first century of the Common Era.

The authority of the rabbi (Hebrew for "my master") also began to develop following the Babylonian exile. Even after Ezra led in the construction of the second Temple in 517–516 B.C.E. (Solomon's Temple had been destroyed 70 years earlier), when the Jews were allowed to return to Israel and resume Temple worship, many chose to remain in exile, in the *galut*. Some Jewish men completely devoted themselves to the study of the Torah and by the first century B.C.E., the rabbinic office had become well-established. The rabbis were not merely teachers, but spiritual authorities for their particular disciples.

During these exilic and post-exilic periods the oral traditions of the rabbis began to gain influence over the life of the ordinary Jew. Although these traditions were not officially compiled until several hundred years later, in a codification called the Talmud, the "Oral Law" was recognized as authoritative for guiding the behavior of Jews well before the days of Yeshua. Remembering that the Oral Law had been around for a while is essential to understanding the *Br'it Chadashah,* the New Covenant, as well as sharing Yeshua with your Jewish neighbor. Many of the questions asked of Yeshua had to do with this oral tradition.

With the rise to power of the Greeks under Alexander the Great, and later the Syrians, the Jews became dominated by other Gentile rulers. In 171 B.C.E. Antiochus IV, the leader of the Syrian-Greeks, began a direct assault on the Jewish way of life. He forbade circumcision and Torah study, and required obeisance to himself by giving himself the title *Epiphanes,* "God-manifest." Many Jews refused to bow down to him. When he sacrificed a pig on the altar in the second Temple and dedicated the altar to the god Jupiter, a group of Jewish people became completely enraged.

A Jewish revolt began in Israel when Mattathias, a righteous priest, slew a fellow Jew for submitting to the ungodly commands of Antiochus. After three years of fighting led by Mattathias' son Judah, the small band of Maccabees ("hammers") led the Jewish people to victory. They purged and rededicated the sacred Temple, which Antiochus had desecrated.

This is the story celebrated today as *Hanukkah,* Hebrew for "dedication." Not only is this battle recorded in the Apocrypha, the non-canonical writings of the Jews of the second Temple period, but the eighth chapter of the prophet Daniel paints a vivid picture of the events leading up to the Maccabean revolt. We know that Yeshua observed the anniversary of this military victory, for John 10:22 records His walking in the Temple at "the Feast of Dedication."

After the cleansing and rededication of the second Temple, two major political/religious parties developed in Israel. One, the party of the scribes, known as Pharisees, were pietistic and separatistic. They began to lose control over the people, while their opponents, the Sadducees, who were more Hellenistic (influenced by Greek thinking), became more powerful. Life in Israel became a real mix of ideas, politics, the supernatural, and the study of the Torah and prophets, combined with the traditions of the rabbis. And on top of this confusion was the increasing control of Rome.

During the first century of the Common Era, Roman rule dominated Jewish history. At the time of Yeshua, the Jews longed for a military Messiah, a hero like Judah Maccabee. It was this desire that caused so many to miss the truth that Yeshua was the Messiah; He just did not fulfill the people's expectation of a military leader. In fact, nothing in Jewish tradition taught that Messiah was to die and be resurrected. That is why He had to teach this to His disciples.

The number of synagogues in Israel had greatly increased by the first century. They were more a place for social gathering and study than for worship and ceremony. The Temple was still the focal point for Jewish worship. But with the complete destruction of the Temple in 70 C.E., some major changes took place.

The synagogue became the place of worship. Those Jews who had chosen to follow Yeshua, having understood Him to be the fulfillment of the ancient sacrificial system of Israel, could not fit in with the new rabbinic religion of Israel. The rabbis attempted to teach alternative means for atonement and to find explanations for the missing Temple. The Jewish believers could not submit to their teaching.

Furthermore, as we have said, Yeshua had warned His disciples to flee from the coming destruction of the Temple and Jerusalem (Matthew 24). Because of His teaching, the believers had removed themselves from a key event of Jewish history. The separation between the Jewish believers in Yeshua and the larger Jewish community was widening.

In 132 C.E., the gap grew greater when the leading rabbi, Rabbi

Akiva, proclaimed Bar Kokhba, a military leader, to be the Messiah. Believing him to be the military hero they sought, the Jewish authorities expected Bar Kokhba to lead the Jews in their revolt against Roman rule. After three years of struggle, this false Messiah lead 580,00 Jews, including himself and Rabbi Akiva, to their deaths.

In 135 C.E., the Romans threw the Jews out of their land, dispersing them throughout the Roman Empire into Spain, Africa, Asia Minor, Europe, and elsewhere. This Diaspora has only really ended in the twentieth century. Keep in mind that some Jews did remain in the land of Israel, mostly in Galilee, but those who remained were very much in the minority from that time forth. Also, there were still Jews living in Babylon (today, Iraq) from the time of the captivity.

According to Solomon Grayzel in *A History of the Jews* (The Jewish Publication Society, Philadelphia, 1970),

> A reasonable guess estimates that there were about eight million Jews in the world just before the conflict with Rome. Probably about one million lived in Babylonia, outside the Roman empire. . . . Thus it has been calculated that in the first century C.E. the Jews were ten per cent of the total population of the Roman empire.

The flight of the Jewish believers at the time of the destruction of the Temple, combined with their unwillingness to submit to rabbinic authority (particularly in the abandoning of the regular Jewish army under Bar Kokhba), caused a permanent and total separation between them and the rest of the Jewish community. We have record of Jewish believers even leading congregations until the Council of Nicea in 325 C.E. After that time and the promulgation of the laws of the Theodosian Code, we see a disappearance of Jewish believers. Since that time, believers in Yeshua have often assimilated into predominantly Gentile congregations.

This information can help you understand and explain why it seems most Jews haven't believed in Yeshua through the ages. The fact is, many have, but because those Jewish believers did not remain part of the Jewish community, no one knew about them. Not until the recent revival among Jewish people and, with it, the rise of the Messianic congregational movement, has the Jewish community become aware that many Jews do believe in Jesus.

## From the Great Dispersion to Today

Because this is a book about sharing the Messiah with Jewish people, and not a modern history of the Jews, I've taken pains to choose those events that will most directly affect your witness. These five major events are: 1) the development of the Talmud and the Jewish religion; 2) the anti-Semitism of the Roman Catholic Church; 3) the immigration of Jews to the United States; 4) the persecution by Nazi Germany; and 5) the rebirth of the nation of Israel.

Our next chapter will discuss the Talmud in light of its impact upon Jewish religion. An earlier chapter spoke about the anti-Semitism of some of the Church fathers and of the Roman Catholic Church. What remains for us here is to consider the immigration of Jews to America, the Holocaust instituted by Nazi Germany, and the rebirth of Israel.

Jewish life in Europe in the second millennium was most unpleasant. Jews, as I said, were accused of causing the Black Death. They were also blamed for many social, financial, and political problems. They began to be "ghetto-ized," forced to live only among themselves.

Religious persecution persisted, and when there was an opportunity to move to America, where freedom seemed a possibility, many Jews packed up all they had, boarded boats, and sailed to the New World.

Although there have been Jews in this country since 1621, the first Jewish settlement wasn't officially established until 1654. As you might guess, it was in New Amsterdam, later known as New York. Soon after, Jews came from other European countries, including Holland, England, Germany, and Spain. They had to struggle for their rights in this new land, but struggle they did. They fought in the American Revolution, won the right to own property, and were granted full U.S. citizenship equal to their Gentile counterparts.

By 1825, the United States had become home for 6,000 Jews. By the Civil War, mostly as a result of immigration, 150,000 Jews lived here. Like other Americans, some fought for the North, some for the South. By 1871, 250,000 Jews, mostly of German background, lived in this country.

During the period from 1881 to 1914, a second wave of Jewish immigration washed across the American shore. These 2,000,000 Jews from Eastern and Central Europe were driven from their homeland by prejudice and pogroms. Most were Yiddish-speaking Orthodox Jews. During World War I, more than 250,000 Jews fought in the armed forces of the United States.

With the Jewish population growing, groups such as the Zionist Organization of America, the American Jewish Committee, the American Jewish Congress, and the Anti-Defamation League of B'nai B'rith were organized to tend to the needs of these new American citizens. The Great Depression brought extra pressure on this poor immigrant people.

Perhaps the single most important factor prompting Jews to escape to America was the rise of Hitler's virulent brand of anti-Semitism in Europe. Seeking safety, thousands of Jews emigrated before the dark days of destruction that began in 1933 when Hitler became dictator of Germany.

Hitler initiated a boycott of Jewish-owned businesses, confiscated the possessions of many Jews, and espoused his racial superiority doctrine. His policies were permitted under the Nuremberg Laws and promulgated by a powerful propaganda machine, particularly through widespread distribution of the newspaper *Der Sturmer*. Hitler reasoned rightly that centuries of anti-Semitic propaganda would sufficiently affect and infect Western minds so that not many who heard of the horror would defend the Jews, no matter what the Nazis did. *The Protocols of the Elders of Zion*, a little booklet first printed in Czarist Russia that Hitler had translated into German, ostensibly detailed a Jewish plot to take over the world. It was later proved to be a fabricated document, but was widely circulated, helping Hitler's cause. Henry Ford was one very influential American who supported the spread of this poisonous propaganda until he later admitted that he had been misled.

The night of November 9–10, 1938, brought with it the horror of *Kristallnacht*, "the night of the broken glass." Hitler's hordes were unleashed; they destroyed synagogues, devastated Jewish shops and homes, and arrested thousands. The world remained silent.

From 1939 until the end of Hitler's horrors, 6,000,000 Jews and an equal number of non-Jews lost their lives under Nazi domination. During this time, from 1933 to 1942, 175,000 Jews from Germany, Austria, and other Nazi-dominated lands escaped to enter the United States. Many more Jews arrived after World War II.

By 1957, the U.S. Jewish population had reached 5,200,000. Today that number is close to 6,000,000, with half living in the Greater New York area. A half-million Jewish people reside in Los Angeles, a third of a million in Philadelphia, and several hundred thousand each in Boston, Chicago, and the Baltimore-Washington areas.

About 3,000,000 Jews, half the size of the U.S. Jewish population, currently reside in Israel and another 3,000,000 remain in the Soviet Union. The other four million Jews are scattered over all parts of the earth. This dispersion can be seen as the fulfillment of the word spoken by Moses: "Moreover, the Lord will scatter you among all peoples, from one end of the earth to the other end of the earth" (Deuteronomy 28:64).

Without question, the single most important event in post-biblical Jewish history has been the rebirth of the state of Israel.

Each year, as Jewish people conclude the Passover meal, they recite the words, "Next year in Jerusalem." The prayer of the Jewish people for 2,000 years, ever since the dispersion began in 135 C.E., has been to celebrate the Passover in Israel. In 1948, this longing became a reality.

Although Jews have inhabited Israel off and on since the dispersion, it wasn't until the late 1800s that the notion of a renewed Jewish state began to receive support. Backed by funds supplied by Baron Edmond de Rothschild, Jews began to establish agricultural communities in Israel. In 1897, at the First Zionist Congress, convened by Theodore Herzl, the World Zionist Organization was founded to establish a homeland for the Jewish people in the land known today as Israel. Herzl was its first president.

Controversy raged within and without the worldwide Jewish community; still Herzl maintained his vision and obtained support for his cause from other leaders. Chaim Weizmann, the fourth president of the World Zionist Organization, was able to persuade England to issue the Balfour Declaration in 1917, approving the idea of a Jewish homeland in "Palestine."

It was not until 1948 that Israel was finally granted full statehood. Great Britain, receiving enormous pressure following World War II, opted to turn over the question of a Jewish state to the United Nations. The U.N. recommended dividing the territory into both Israeli and Arab states. On May 14, 1948, Israel became a nation for the first time in modern history.

Although Israel has had to defend herself in numerous wars since 1948, it appears that in God's timing, the day for Israel to exist as a nation has come. It is a modern miracle that such a small country, vastly outnumbered by surrounding enemies, survives. We who believe in Yeshua see this as God's hand protecting His people.

This skeletal report on 4,000 years of Jewish history has been designed to provide you with information to enhance your understanding of your Jewish neighbor. The next chapters will flesh out our skeleton by offering insight into the religion and culture of the Jewish people. Tied very closely to the history that has been outlined thus far, you will see the details of the completed picture come to life as we proceed.

# 10

# The Religion of the Jewish People
## —or—
### *The Three T's: Torah, Temple, and Talmud*

In the study of civilizations it is usually quite difficult to separate history from religion. For the Jewish people it is impossible. Why? Because the Jews were created with religion in mind. When God formed this particular people, His intention was that they would teach the world about Him. From the beginning, the history and religion of the Jewish people were intertwined the way ivy crawls up and amidst the branches of a tree.

The last chapter briefly surveyed the history of the Jewish people, from God's ancient covenant with Abraham to the establishment of the modern State of Israel. Throughout, there were references to religion. This chapter will highlight the religion of the Jewish people from Bible times, through its development over the last two millennia, and as it is practiced today.

## From Abraham to the Great Dispersion

From the time of Abraham until the giving of God's Law through Moses, the religion of Israel was rather primitive. Altars of stone were erected to commemorate certain divine interventions by the Lord. We think, for example, of Abram building an altar to the Lord upon receiving the promise of the land to be given to his descendants (Genesis 12:7). This practice seems rudimentary, but it was a great step from the polytheism that marked the times.

With the revelation of the Torah on Sinai, Israel's religion became oriented toward social relationships and the worship of God. The system of sacrifice grew more developed. Through the Tabernacle and its later replacement, the Temple, God revealed to His people an earthly picture of the heavenly courts (Hebrews 9:23).

Then Solomon's Temple was destroyed and the Jews were taken into captivity (586 B.C.E.). Religion changed drastically. As the review of history indicated, the center of religious life now shifted. The scribes and their teachings dominated for nearly a century until the building of the second Temple, when emphasis once again returned to the ancient system of sacrifice prescribed by Moses. But by the time the new Temple had been completed, the priesthood had taken on the nuances of a political rather than a religious office.

Amidst these changes, the rabbis gained greater authority. Various schools of religious philosophy developed and the Jewish people found themselves divided, as individuals allied themselves with one school or the other, so that by 100 B.C.E. there were Pharisees, Sadducees, Essenes, and more.

The New Covenant talks much about the Pharisees and the Sadducees who struggled continually for power. The Pharisees were more flexible with regard to interpreting the Word of God, whereas the Sadducees were more literal in their interpretations, more rigid in their rules. The Pharisees believed in the reality of the supernatural, while the Sadducees denied it. An example of the divergence of views can be found in the question of the resurrection, in which the Pharisees believed, but the Sadducees did not (Matthew 22:23–33).

Another religious sect was known as the Essenes. In many ways they had much in common with the early believers in the Messiah, particularly in that they shared all their earthly possessions. This separatist group was "heavenly" minded, but most likely did not follow Yeshua. Many scholars believe that the Essenes were the people responsible for what are now called the Dead Sea Scrolls, which came from the Qumran community. Some have suggested that John (Yochanan, in Hebrew) the Immerser was a member of the Essenes.

In addition to these religious sects, there was also a party known as the Zealots. They were not truly religious, except in their dedication to overthrowing the Roman rule over Israel.

Judaism in the first century, and even somewhat earlier, had no clear-cut theology. Although many beliefs were held in common, there were also many variant points of view.

One conviction that many held in common, however, was that Jesus was not the Messiah. Those who believed in Him were considered a separate sect and were sometimes called "Nazarenes," sometimes "the Way," and sometimes "Christians" (although that term seemed to be reserved mostly for Gentile followers of the Messiah).

## From the Great Dispersion of Modern Times

The last chapter mentioned the Talmud. More than anything else, this collection of writings influenced the religion of the Jewish people. In many ways, it *was* the religion of the Jewish people.

Referred to as the Oral Law, the Talmud is believed by many to have been handed down on Sinai along with the written Law, the Torah. As a result it has exerted dominance in matters of religion.

The traditions and commentaries that later became the Talmud trace their roots back into early Jewish history. Tradition teaches that Moses himself first received these oral laws, then passed them on to Joshua who, in turn, handed them down to the elders (the judges). Then the laws were delivered to the prophets who handed them over to the care of the Great Assembly, 120 leaders who returned from exile under the leadership of Ezra. This is according to *Avot* (a tractate of the Talmud) chapter 1, *Mishnah* 1. Finally the laws arrived in the hands of the rabbis.

Rabbi Akiva was responsible for organizing much of this oral material shortly after the time of the New Covenant. The writing, however, is credited to another, Rabbi Judah ha Nasi. His work, known as the Mishnah, forms the foundation of what later became known as the Talmud. The Mishnah is not a commentary on the Bible, but rather is material organized in six sections, called Orders, which discuss various issues in the Bible and Jewish life. The teachers of Mishnah, called *Tannaim,* completed their work around the end of the second century.

The rest of the Talmud, known as *Gemara,* was not completed until the end of the fifth century of the Common Era. The Gemara contains discussions concerning the Mishnah, conducted by the Amoraim, also Jewish scholars.

This entire system is predicated on the theory that God revealed the Oral Law to Moses as well as the written Law. Although it is rare to meet someone today who holds to this elevated view of the Talmud, the impact of the traditions and teachings of the Tannaim and the Amoraim must not be underestimated. These teachers endeavored to construct a fence around the Torah to keep their people from violating the laws of Moses. The legal system became so cumbersome that rabbis were continually called upon to decide legal issues. That is why rabbis are sometimes called "lawyers" in the New Covenant.

In theory, the idea that the rabbis had was a good one. Sadly, though, people became entangled in the multitude of rules and religious regulations so that some of the essential meanings in the Torah became lost. Traditions overshadowed truths.

Yeshua often spoke about this problem. In the Sermon on the Mount, He prefaced His "You have heard it said" remarks by instructing His disciples to exceed the righteousness of the scribes and the Pharisees. Stating specifically that He had come not to abolish the Law and the prophets, but rather to fulfill them, Yeshua then launched into a sermon on the essence of the Law. One can't help but think that Yeshua's concern was to confront the teachings of the oral tradition and to call His disciples to the deeper meaning of the Torah.

But the influence of the Talmud grew still greater. There was a Talmud in Jerusalem and a Talmud in Babylon. Through the last 2,000 years, study of Talmud has been considered one of the noblest and highest endeavors to which a Jewish boy could commit himself. Its study has occupied the greatest minds of the Jewish people. Much can be learned about the Bible from studying the writings in the Talmud. Much can be learned about Jewish history by reading the many debates and discussions recorded there. Unfortunately, even though some of the material found in the Talmud points to the Messiah, to a great extent its writings have obscured the Messiah from many Jewish eyes.

## Modern Times

Early Jewish settlers in the United States formed synagogues in which to worship. The first was founded in Newport, Rhode Island, in 1658. Later, synagogues were established in Savannah, Philadelphia, Charleston, and throughout the thirteen colonies. These were Orthodox synagogues, because at that time no other branch of Judaism existed.

As the German Jews arrived in the mid-1800s they brought with them the influence that became Reform Judaism. In 1875 the Reform movement established Hebrew Union College, the first U.S. rabbinical seminary, in Cincinnati, Ohio.

In 1886 the Jewish Theological Seminary of America was formed. From its teachings sprang another movement, known as Conservative Judaism. Reform Judaism, the most liberal branch, gleans some of its ideology from the higher criticism of the German intellectual community, the same higher criticism that gave birth to the liberal movement within Christianity. Conservative Judaism, on the other hand, rose up to moderate the Reform movement. It is theologically more conservative, more middle-of-the-road.

The fourth branch of Judaism is known as Reconstructionism. Originated by Mordecai Kaplan in 1934, it teaches that Judaism is more than a religion: It is a religious civilization. Although smaller in numbers than the other branches, Reconstructionism has some strong support within the intellectual circles of the Jewish people.

Orthodox Jews strive to keep the laws and traditions of Judaism with great zeal. They express an expectancy of the coming Messiah. They believe in an afterlife and consider the Torah and Talmud to be the Word of God.

Reform Jews tend to liberalize laws and traditions, picking and choosing what they wish to believe and observe in today's world. They do not teach about the coming Messiah, but have opted instead for the concept of the Messianic age, a higher plane, and a time of peace, into which they believe we are evolving.

Conservatism follows the teachings of the rabbis but allows for certain modifications to make tradition fit into the society in which it is practiced. For example, whereas Orthodox Jews do not allow men and women to sit together in the synagogue, Conservative Jews do. This middle-of-the-road position also guides their views pertaining to the Messiah and the afterlife.

Reconstructionist Jews, like Conservative Jews, seek to adapt Judaism to the world in which it must function. To this end Reconstructionist Jews, *unlike* Conservative Jews, incorporate modern secular thought in the services of their synagogues. They are drawn to such concepts as ethical culture, ritual enrichment, and artistic creativity.

It will help you in your witness to know a little about the various branches of Judaism, though you should not necessarily conclude that your neighbor buys into all the doctrines espoused by the synagogue to which he belongs. As is the case with many Christians, Jewish people often join synagogues, not so much because of theology, but because of proximity and personality. When you are getting to know your neighbor, at some point you'll want to ask what exactly he or she believes personally.

The glossary at the end of this book lists terms that pertain to the religious observance of the Jewish people. You will find that no matter which branch of Judaism your Jewish neighbor belongs to, most of the terms are relevant to one degree or another. Take, for example, the term *kosher*. Generally, only the Orthodox and some Conservative Jews "keep kosher." Still, all Jews have some way of dealing with the subject. You'll find this to be true for nearly every aspect of Jewish life.

Just as the history of the Jews is intertwined with the theology of the Jews, both are intertwined with the rich and fascinating culture of the Jewish people, which we will take time to examine now.

# 11

## Jewish Culture
## —or—
## *Celebrating, Jewish Style*

No people, other than the Jews, were ever formed with the express purpose of being a continual testimony to the existence of God. No other people were gathered together to teach the truths of the Almighty. No other people were created to receive His words, inscribed upon tablets of stone. Because of this uniqueness, the history, religion, and culture of the Jewish people have been and always will be intertwined.

Despite this singleness of purpose, however, God has allowed for a great deal of diversity among the Jewish people. As someone has said, when you gather four Jews together to discuss a matter, you will invariably end up with five opinions!

To begin with, Jews trace their origins to two major groups, the *Ashkenazim* and *Sephardim*. *Ashkenazi* Jews came to America from the Eastern European nations and tend to be fairer-skinned. *Sephardic* Jews hail from the Mediterranean countries and are darker. The stereotypical native-born Israeli, or *sabra,* with his olive complexion, black, curly hair, and dark, soulful eyes is a picture of the *Sephardic* Jew. (*Sabra* is the name of an Israeli desert plant. Tough on the outside and tender on the inside. This is how the Israeli sees himself.)

Each of the two major groups, *Ashkenazim* and *Sephardim,* has its own traditions and customs. To understand your Jewish neighbor better, ask questions about his or her background.

Additional diversity can be seen in politics. Traditionally, Jews in America have tended toward a socially liberal philosophy and membership in the Democratic party. Through the years, the Democratic party seemed most sensitive to the needs of immigrants and aid to the downtrodden. Jews, previous to the last two generations, have for the most part fallen into both of these categories. There still is a leaning toward the left, although as Jews have become more established within American society, we find that they are slowly drifting toward a more conservative point of view.

Regarding Israel, you will also find a variety of views. Some American Jews have become critical of the ways of the Jews living in the land. Others hold fast to an "Israel, right or wrong" position. But one thing the vast majority of Jews agree on is the need for keeping Israel strong. The fact is, it was only a generation ago that Hitler led a "civilized" nation to exterminate 6,000,000 Jews. That vivid memory keeps Jewish people acutely aware of how important a homeland is, one in which they would be willing to make their last stand if necessary.

You may not agree with the politics of Israel, or the way things are done there. But, as a Bible-believer, you must speak to your Jewish neighbor about Israel in a noncritical, supportive way. Just as people bristle when they hear others speak badly of their mothers, Jews don't like to hear Gentiles speak badly about their motherland. Jewish people may vary when it comes to ethnic background or political views, but on the subject of Israel's survival, you will find Jews strongly united.

At the risk of sounding redundant, there is something else all Jewish people have shared: persecution. From Abraham onward, Jews have had to struggle to survive. Modern history has found Jews forced to live in ghettos set apart specifically for Jews to occupy. In Eastern Europe, these little towns were called *shtetls*. Jews knew that safety could be found only within the environs of the *shtetl*. Outside of the village lay danger. It was easy to divide the world into those two categories: "us" and "them."

This "us/them" mentality makes it hard at times for Jews to trust "outsiders." The truth is, many Jews, deep within, still have a basic fear of other people. This makes your witness harder. You are most likely going to be perceived as a "them." Remember our chapter on credibility: A key factor is identification. It will help your witness if you can learn and appreciate the culture of your Jewish neighbor.

Appreciating Jewish food, humor, music, and other aspects of culture should not be a tough assignment. You will most likely enjoy and appreciate some of the things that make us "us"! One thing is for certain, Jewish people love to celebrate.

When a young churchgoer is confirmed, the event is often celebrated by serving cookies, cakes, coffee, and punch in the church social hall following the service. Contrast this with the Jewish "confirmation" known as a Bar Mitzvah.

The Bar Mitzvah is, as we have seen, a legal rite of passage for a thirteen-year-old boy. Standing before the synagogue he is asked to perform the adult role in the service, reading from the Tenakh, chanting the blessings, giving a little *drush*, a short sermon. In times past, following the service, the parents would provide a traditional light meal served in honor of the Bar Mitzvah boy.

But in recent years, the Bar Mitzvah has become more than a rite of passage for the boy. It has become an occasion for gala celebration. Jewish history, fraught with catastrophe and turmoil, has caused Jewish people to look forward to such joyous occasions.

Today the Bar Mitzvah party is a first-class catered event to which relatives from far and near are invited. Beginning in the evening, eating, drinking, dancing, and general revelry carry on nonstop until the early hours of the morning. The Bar Mitzvah is just one example of how Gentile culture differs from Jewish culture and how Jewish history and religion have had a thorough impact on it. You will probably become aware of these cultural differences as you get to know your Jewish neighbor. You may even enjoy them!

You can also learn to value what Jewish people value. Jews do place a heavy emphasis on education. Maybe it comes from starting out as the people of the Book, but higher education has always been prized, something to sacrifice for, something looked upon as a worthy achievement.

Family, too, has traditionally been a high priority among the Jews. Going back to the Torah we find some instruction that has elevated the importance of family. The Lord told the Jewish people, "Honor your father and your mother, that your days may be prolonged in the land which the Lord your God gives you" (Exodus 20:12). He also instructed Israel to "teach them [the commandments] diligently to your sons and . . . talk of them when you sit in your house and when you walk by the way and when you lie down and when you rise up" (Deuteronomy 6:7). This emphasis on family has kept the Jewish people relatively exempt from the temptations of the world. Until recently.

Today, not unlike what is going on in the rest of the world, more and more Jewish couples are getting divorced and Jewish teenagers are as susceptible to drugs as any other kids. You may find that your faith can be a beacon, a beacon that might draw your Jewish neighbor back to the biblical values that are at the heart of his own cultural distinctives.

A few other cultural aspects of Jewish life also find their roots in the religion of the Jewish people—dietary laws, births, deaths, and holidays.

*Kashrut,* or kosher, means "in alignment with religious law," proper, fit. Many things can be considered kosher—a Torah, an action, a prayer shawl. But when you hear about it, you're probably thinking about food, for that is its most common application.

There are many laws of *kashrut.* How an animal should be killed. How an animal should not be cooked. What animals are considered "fit." The laws God gave to the Jews were to set them apart as a holy people. He didn't want His chosen ones mixing in with the pagans and their pagan practices. The dietary laws did much to distinguish the Jews from the non-Jews, and thus kept His people unique.

Although there are many specific biblical commands concerning *kashrut,* many additional traditions developed surrounding them. To give you an example of how the Talmud and traditions have worked, let's look at one kosher law.

Deuteronomy 14:21c reads, "You shall not boil a kid in its mother's milk." God didn't want His people boiling baby goats in their own mother's milk. From this commandment, religious Jewish people have ended up with two sets of dishes for meals—one for meat products, one for milk or dairy products.

The rabbis, zealous to make certain that no one inadvertently cooked a baby goat in its mother's milk, set forth this law of the separate dishes. It was this same zeal that led them to state that separate sets of dishes were needed exclusively for Passover to ensure that there be no chance of eating leavened bread, since it was unkosher to do so during the Passover week.

This all might sound a little much, and perhaps it is somewhat excessive, but the initial idea to put a "fence around the Law" was a plan to make it harder to break God's commandments. The fence was composed of tradition. Tradition became such a strong force in the life of the Jewish community that we hear the character Tevye in *Fiddler on the Roof* offer it as the reason Jewish people were able to keep their balance. "Without tradition," he explains, "our lives would be as shaky as a fiddler on the roof!"

Your Jewish friend may or may not keep kosher. He or she might keep biblically kosher. He or she might keep traditionally kosher. At home the laws of *kashrut* might be kept. In a Chinese restaurant they might be suspended.

Once again, you can see that the cultural adaptations of the religious precepts vary from person to person. Some Jews won't eat pork, but use only one set of dishes. Others might keep all leaven out of their homes during Passover, but order shrimp if they go out to dinner. As with other ways of my Jewish people, there are a lot of varieties on the kosher theme. Taking time to talk to your Jewish neighbor about his or her ideas concerning *kashrut* is the best way to gain understanding.

Another cultural event that finds its roots in Scripture is birth. All of us celebrate the birth of a newborn baby. It is one of the most exquisitely awesome events in life. Jewish people have a unique ceremony surrounding the birth of a baby boy. It is called *Br'it Milah,* the Covenant of Circumcision, and it is at this ceremony that the baby is named. This ancient practice goes back to the days of Abraham. Circumcision was to be a sign of the covenant God made with the Jewish people and was to be performed on each male when he was eight days old (Genesis 17:10–14).

Luke 2:21 (KJV) records Yeshua's circumcision and naming:

> And when eight days were accomplished for the circumcising of the child, his name was called Jesus [Yeshua], which was so named of the angel before he was conceived in the womb.

I realize there is some debate today concerning the subject of circumcision. Is it good for Gentiles to circumcise their sons? Should believers, Jewish or Gentile, circumcise their sons, given Paul's thoughts on the subject? Is it an old-fashioned ceremony that should be avoided because it might be traumatic for the infant?

For the purposes of our discussion you need simply to be aware that at the birth of a son and the circumcision and naming that follow, a major event is taking place. Obviously, this is not the time to discuss circumcision in light of New Covenant information. Rather, congratulate the parents that their son has been given the sign of the covenant God gave to the Jewish people, and to those who allied themselves with Israel.

The naming ceremony has variations. As in the Bible, a baby boy or girl is named "So-and-so," son or daughter of "So-and-so." This was readily seen when Yeshua called His disciple *Simon bar Jonah*, meaning *Simon son of Jonah*. If the baby is a girl, she would be a *bat* (daughter), not a *bar* (son). That's why girls have Bat Mitzvah celebrations, rather than Bar Mitzvah celebrations. They are "daughters of the commandment."

The Jewish people you are likely to meet will not be known by these Hebrew names. Since Jews have lived in the lands of others since the dispersion, they have adopted names popular in the lands in which they live. My name *Barry*, for example, is quite Anglo-Saxon. The name I was given at my circumcision, *Baruch*, Hebrew for "blessed," is rarely used. Only a few of my closest family and friends ever call me this. In America I am Barry. But if I were to live in Israel, I'd be *Baruch*.

By the way, in case you're interested, my full Hebrew name is *Baruch ben Israel*, "blessed son of Israel." *Ben* also means "son" and my father's Hebrew name was *Israel*. This never meant more to me than when I became a follower of the true Son of Israel, Yeshua the Messiah. Actually, I, like most *Ashkenazim*, was named after a deceased relative. This tradition was developed to memorialize the dead through the living.

Knowing about these auspicious occasions, the birth, circumcision, and naming of a Jewish child, will give you an opportunity to converse in an intelligent way. You can inquire about the name and what it means. You can ask about the deceased person who is being memorialized. You can even send a card or gift. It is one of those times when you can really show your love and friendship.

Another time in which you can become closer to your Jewish friend is at the Bar or Bat Mitzvah. We've already looked a little at this ceremony that takes place at age thirteen, comparing it with a Christian confirmation. But a few other insights will help you identify with your Jewish friend.

The typical Bar or Bat Mitzvah is held in a synagogue on Saturday morning. The child is actually treated as an adult and asked to participate in the regular service. Generally, after the ceremony, there is an elaborate *kiddush,* a spread of food that you wouldn't want to miss. If you are ever invited, definitely go. Not only would you be showing your support for your friend's culture and Jewishness, but you'll be treating yourself to a great time. The service is generally longer than your average church service, but I think you'll find it fascinating. Remember, Yeshua went to synagogue; there were no churches.

As I described before, there is quite a party in the evening. It usually costs a great deal so often just family and closest friends are invited. If you are invited, consider it a great honor and go. You may not drink alcoholic beverages or believe in dancing—there will be both at this bash—but not going might offend your Jewish friend. Oh, you should also bring a very nice gift. Often guests give the Bar Mitzvah boy or Bat Mitzvah girl a generous check.

Another event in the life of your Jewish friend that is especially meaningful is a wedding. Even though Jewish weddings have similarities to Christian weddings, there are a few differences of which you should be aware. If you go to your Jewish friend's wedding, or the wedding of his or her child, you may see some unusual ceremonies.

To begin with, often the parents of both the bride and groom walk their respective children down the aisle. By doing so they symbolize the concept of both man and woman leaving their fathers and mothers.

You will see the two who are getting married standing under a canopy, called a *hupah,* which symbolizes the consummation of marriage. In biblical times, a man brought a woman into his tent, consummated their relationship, and then they were married. Since tents often symbolize God's covering of His people, I like to see the *hupah* as standing for God's covering of this union.

Once under the canopy, the rabbi will ask the groom to repeat the following: "Be sanctified [set apart] to me with this ring in accordance with the Law of Moses and Israel." You may also hear the reading of the *ketubah,* or marriage contract. This, written prior to the ceremony, is the promise made by the groom to support and care for his wife. The *Sheva Brakhot,* the Seven Benedictions, are usually chanted in Hebrew by the cantor or rabbi.

At the culmination of the ceremony, it is customary to place a small glass on the floor for the groom to step on and break. The breaking of the glass has several traditional derivations, but the most prevalent one is that it commemorates the destruction of the Temple in 70 c.e. Those who understand the meaning are reminded that Judaism is incomplete without the Temple. We Jewish believers in Yeshua see that biblical Judaism was fulfilled in the atoning work of the Messiah.

Then comes the party. Since a wedding is a *simcha,* a celebration, it behooves guests to have fun. So if you are attending a Jewish wedding, enjoy yourself! Eat, sing, dance as long as you don't have a conviction against it (and you're not on a diet!). Remember, Paul said to the Jews he became as a Jew. So enjoy.

At the birth of a baby, the Bar Mitzvah of a boy, or the marriage of a couple, you have a wonderful opportunity to grow closer to your Jewish neighbor. These occasions give you a chance to show your identification and concern for your Jewish friend. But there is no time in which to draw closer than following the death of your friend's loved one.

To a believer, death means absent from the body, present with the Lord. We miss the one who died but have the assurance that he or she is in a far better place. For Jewish people who don't believe, death is desperately depressing. Jewish funerals are sad affairs. Jewish people today are without a real hope in an afterlife. So questions about the futility of life flood the mind. Some Jewish people do hold a somewhat superstitious view of life beyond death, but it seems to me that most consider death the end, not the beginning.

The first seven-day period after the burial of a relative (burials are to be done as soon after death as possible) is called *shiva* (seven). During this time the family will wear an item of torn clothing. (In the Bible when people mourned, they would rend, or tear, their garments.) Mourners sit on low stools or boxes, not normal chairs. Some actually sit on the floor, which is where the expression *sitting shiva* comes from. No leather shoes are worn. Shaving or hair-cutting is not permitted, nor is the use of cosmetics. None of the usual pleasures of life is to be enjoyed.

It is customary during this period to visit the mourning family in the home where they are sitting *shiva*. However, since words cannot adequately express the grief the mourner is feeling, visitors are generally asked not to say anything to those mourning unless spoken to. It is also customary to allow fond discussion of the deceased if the mourner mentions the one who died. This aids the mourner through the period of mourning.

Two other periods of mourning, one lasting for thirty days following the date of death, the other until the one-year anniversary, complete the mourning period.

If you are close enough to your Jewish friend, you can visit the "*shiva* house." Be *with* your Jewish friend, letting him or her talk about the loss just experienced. It would not be in good taste to talk about the afterlife at this time, no matter what is being said. This is a time simply to recognize the sovereignty of God and emphasize God's mercy and compassion. It is not a time to discuss judgment, atonement, salvation, heaven, or hell. Your ministry to your Jewish friend should be one of comfort and consolation. Pray the Comforter can give you words to console your Jewish neighbor.

Understanding the cultural uniqueness of your Jewish friend will go a long way toward introducing him or her to the Messiah. You will not only understand your audience, but you will grow closer as people. It is important that you build a relationship of trust, confidence, and friendship with the person with whom you want to share. Leave the pulpit-pounding to others. You need to be a friend, ready, willing, and able to love your Jewish neighbor. The glossary on pp. 197–201 offers you more information about the history, religion, and culture of the Jewish people that may be helpful to you in your witness.

# SECTION IV

## Feedback: Barriers to Belief

Once I watched two Jewish men debate the Messiahship of Jesus. One was a believer, the other was not. On the surface such debates sound worthwhile, but argumentation often leads to anger, which is what happened in this case. Assessing the impact of the debate (and there have been many such debates in history), I concluded that nothing was accomplished. Nothing, that is, except to show two Jews fighting one another.

I recount that story to you because in this section we are going to discuss barriers to belief. Although you might feel equipped to win debates, let me offer you a suggestion.

One of the traps we fall into is to suppose that all we must do is present a clear case for the Messiah and people will believe. Unfortunately, this is not true. Scripture teaches us that God's Spirit is responsible for drawing individuals to the Messiah. Faith is a gift from God.

You might ask, then, "How do I begin sharing my faith?" The answer is easy. Clear away the clumps. The following illustration will help you understand.

Several years ago I tried my hand at gardening. I knew next to nothing about it. But I asked around, read a little, and set out to see if my thumb was green. It wasn't, but I learned some valuable lessons in the process.

I learned most of all about clump-clearing. The soil in which I was attempting to garden was one big lump of clay, hard as a rock. All the books I read on the subject told me that the soil had to be broken up, that the clumps had to be cleared out. I spent hours and hours chopping away at those large chunks. It almost broke my back!

Later, I noticed that the seeds I had planted in the areas prepared most diligently grew. The ones I had put in soil less rigorously primed hardly grew at all. The seeds contained within them the potential for life. My part in the process had been to encourage that life to take root.

This section comes under the heading of clump-clearing— breaking through barriers to belief. Your Jewish neighbor may be a seed waiting to germinate. By learning how to break through barriers to belief, you can encourage the seed to grow. It is the work of God's Spirit to draw the person to Him. Your job is simply to start breaking up the ground and clearing out the clumps.

You will see from the witnessing model at the beginning of this section that we have arrived at the final point in the communication process. It is called Feedback, your Jewish neighbor's response. You already have a good sense of who you are and how you may be perceived. We have discussed what the "Jewish Gospel" is all about, and you have a better idea about what your Jewish neighbor is likely to believe, think, and feel. Let's begin to discuss just what clumps you are likely to encounter as you start plowing up the soil, preparing it for the Gospel seed to be planted in the heart of your Jewish neighbor.

This section divides those barriers into three categories: historical, theological, and personal. Understanding why these barriers have been erected and knowing how to break through them will equip you to enable your Jewish neighbor to meet his or her Messiah.

# 12

## The Art of Discernment
### —or—
### *When Is a Question Not a Question? That is the Question*

Soon you'll become familiar with the historical, theological, and personal barriers to belief that might keep the Gospel seed from taking root. You will also be supplied with the tools necessary to break down those barriers. But before we get into that, let's see what the Messiah has to say on the subject.

When Yeshua sent out the twelve disciples He instructed them carefully: "Behold, I send you out as sheep in the midst of wolves; therefore be shrewd as serpents, and innocent as doves" (Matthew 10:16). He was warning His disciples to be alert when they went out as His representatives. He wasn't calling His own Jewish people "wolves." Remember He was speaking to Jews, as well as about some of them. You need not be worried that your Jewish neighbor is a wolf whom you should fear. You won't face the same danger as did the disciples. Most Jewish people are kind and thoughtful people.

Nevertheless, Yeshua's advice is worth heeding. Be shrewd as serpents and innocent as doves. Be discerning in your witness, especially when it comes to answering questions.

There are many different kinds of questions. Some are asked to gain information. Others have different intentions.

Have you ever listened to a call-in radio show on which an expert was available to answer questions? You've probably noticed how many of those questions aren't really questions at all. Sometimes they appear as questions but are really statements. Sometimes they are challenges disguised as questions. Sometimes they are asked only so a person can hear himself talk.

When I first began teaching in a college I didn't have much discernment. Often students would raise their hands, ostensibly to ask a question or receive clarification. After listening for a while, I would offer what I considered to be an appropriate answer, only to find out that the question was not a question at all. The more experience I had, the more I realized that occasionally a questioner would use his or her question time to give a little speech. The longer I taught, the more adept I became at distinguishing true questions.

I developed a little discernment. Sometimes I was even able to hear the questions that lay behind the question.

Talking with people about the Messiah likewise requires some degree of discernment. Occasionally, a question may be raised for the purpose of challenging what you say. Sometimes the question is designed just to throw another clump, even a boulder, into your garden. Sometimes a question might simply be a way of expressing personal feelings. Experience, coupled with prayer for discernment, will help you sense the purpose that often lies behind the question.

One characteristic of the communication style of Jewish people is to answer one question with another. For instance:

"So, Bernie, how's your daughter?"

" 'How's my daughter?' you ask. How do you think she is with five kids?"

Or:

"Dad, do you think you could get me a new car?"

"A new car? Do I look like I'm made of money?"

Both of the responses to the questions are really answers combined with statements. When, where, or how this style of communicating began is hard to say. But does it exist among the Jewish people? Would I lie about such a thing?

Whenever it began, some similar system was already in place at the time of Yeshua. He also answered questions with questions. You will see this as we go through this chapter.

In order for you to be more effective in communicating the Good News that Messiah has come, here are a few examples of Jesus' communication style. They show you how He answered a question with a question—how He applied principles of discernment.

## The Challenging Question (Matthew 21:23–27)

The chief priests and elders of the people came to Yeshua and asked Him by what authority He taught. From a human point of view, they had every right to pose this question because they were responsible for the care of the people. Yeshua's authority came from the Father and obviously exceeded theirs, but He wasn't ready to reveal this to them. He wanted to avoid responding directly. He did so by answering a question with a question.

He asked the chief priests a question He knew they wouldn't want to answer. He promised that if they first answered His question, He would respond to theirs. Before responding to their challenge, He placed the chief priests in the position of having to admit that John the Immerser had received his authority from heaven. If they refused to acknowledge this, the chief priests would arouse the anger of those who believed John to be a prophet.

Yeshua wasn't trying to make trouble. He was avoiding confrontation and challenge, and facing them with the insincerity of their position.

When you talk with your Jewish friend about Jewish things, you might find yourself challenged. It might help you understand what I mean if I share some of the challenging questions we have heard in this ministry:

"Who gave you the right to tell me that Jesus is the Messiah?"

"Do you know Hebrew?"

"Have you been to rabbinical school?"

Are these really questions? Not really. They are challenges. It might be wise, in such cases, to avoid answering them. Proverbs 26:5 says, "Answer a fool as his folly deserves, lest he be wise in his own eyes." Let's examine, for a moment, some ways you might answer the challenging question.

Suppose you were able to say honestly, "Yes, I speak fluent Hebrew and have recently graduated from rabbinical school." Do you think that would satisfy your Jewish friend? Do you suppose that would persuade him that your point of view had suddenly become more tenable? Don't assume it for a moment! His response to your impressive credentials might likely be a flippant, "Well, you certainly didn't learn very much in rabbinical school," or even, "With such a fine education, why waste your time trying to convert Jews?" Again, these responses come from real conversations.

Chances are you won't hear these statements often, simply because you're not a "professional missionary," just a concerned friend. But I offer these to you as examples of challenges dressed up as questions. Pray for discernment and you will begin to detect the difference between what is sincere and what is merely designed to get you off the Gospel track.

Yeshua's approach was to sidestep the challenging question by answering with another question. If your Jewish neighbor challenges you saying, "Do you speak Hebrew?" or "Have you been to rabbinical school?" try answering with a question such as, "If I *did* speak Hebrew or if I *had* been to rabbinical school, would you be more open to believing that Yeshua might be the Messiah?" It might help your Jewish friend realize that he is really just challenging your right to share your faith with him. Again, let me reiterate that you will probably not be challenged the way workers in Jewish ministries have been. None of your Jewish neighbors is going to expect that you've been to rabbinical school or are a Hebraicist. I just want you to see that sometimes a challenging statement comes dressed up as a question.

Remember, your right to share comes from a higher Authority. That you don't speak Hebrew and that you have not been to rabbinical school has nothing to do with the fact that God has revealed to you the truth of His Messiah. But stating so in a forthright way might not be timely to do at this point in your witness. So, be discerning like Yeshua. Consider sidestepping the challenging question.

## The Trap Question (Matthew 22:15–22)

Matthew tells us that the Pharisees counseled together in order to entangle or trap Yeshua. They sent out their disciples with some Herodians, the political party that supported King Herod. After complimenting Yeshua—"Master, we know You are truthful and teach the way of God in truth . . ."—they set their trap. "Tell us what You think. Is it lawful to give tribute to Caesar, or not?"

They were trying to cause Him to alienate Himself from either the common people or the Roman rulers. Either answer would have resulted in serious repercussions. Had Yeshua admitted that it was lawful to pay tribute to Caesar, the commoners, already heavily taxed, would have muttered resentment. If, on the other hand,

Yeshua had declared it unlawful, He would have been in trouble with the government.

Once again, Yeshua answered their question with one of His own: "Whose image and superscription is on the denarius?" The answer was plain: "Caesar's." "Then," He said, "render to Caesar the things that are Caesar's, and to God the things that are God's." He never really said whether or not it was lawful. He captured reality and gave no offense to either group.

Your Jewish neighbor might ask, "Do you support Israel?" This can be as loaded a question as the one posed to Yeshua years ago. Your Jewish neighbor knows that things are not perfect in the land, but there is another issue behind your Jewish neighbor's question that goes beyond current events. It is the issue of whether or not you can be trusted. Are you a friend of the Jewish people, or not? Are you an "us" or a "them"?

Israel is the Jewish homeland. In the back of the minds of many Jews is the notion that someday they might choose to (or be forced to) live there. Your answer to his question, "Do you support Israel?" will reveal a lot about you and about the faith that you are espousing. Are you to be considered trustworthy (remember our discussion on credibility)? Is what you're sharing about Yeshua safe to listen to?

Most believers I know support Israel because of what the Bible says. Not only must Jews be living in the land before the return of the Messiah, but God guaranteed it to be a homeland for His people. Most believers would answer, "Yes, I support Israel."

There are, however, American Jewish people who find themselves on the horns of a dilemma. Some are embarrassed and concerned by the media's reporting of the recurring Palestinian problem. They don't want Israel to be or appear to be violent. Yet, to be too critical about Israel means speaking against the "homeland."

Others support a strong stand concerning the unrest on the West Bank. Some would like to move all Palestinians out of the land, period. American Jews have strong feelings on both sides of the issue about Israel. Some have expressed themselves in critical terms. Others are more supportive. What you need to remember is that it's the *Jewish* homeland that Jews are arguing about. In many ways it's a family matter.

Your answer to the question, "Do you support Israel?" will require discernment. Instead of offering a quick yes or no, why not use this opportunity to clarify your position? You can present the biblical view that God promised the land to the Jewish people (Genesis 13:14–15; 15:18–21; 26:1–5; 28:1–4). Explain that you are looking for the day when there will be lasting peace in the land—the day when the Messiah returns to set up His Millennium of peace. You can express some thoughts about how sad you are to see young Palestinian and Jewish children hurt. Do not feel trapped into giving a quick yes or no when more explanation is needed.

It might not be the intention of your Jewish neighbor to trap you as the Pharisees tried to ensnare Yeshua. Still, the question might be unintentionally loaded. By avoiding the trap of feeling constrained to an unequivocal yes or no, you may effectively use the opportunity to explain the real answer, that peace will not come until Yeshua does. Your witness will be stronger for it.

## The False Question (Matthew 22:23–33)

Matthew tells us that later that day, after Yeshua had dealt with the Pharisees, He was visited by the Sadducees who presented Him with a false question.

The subject was resurrection, something that Yeshua had taught His disciples. But here He was faced by the Sadducees, the sect of Jews that did not believe in the resurrection. Their question was complex and intentionally sticky. They proposed a hypothetical situation. Suppose a man were to die and his younger brother, following the Torah (Deuteronomy 25:5), were to marry the dead man's wife. Then suppose this man died and his next younger brother married the wife. Then suppose this happened to all seven brothers in the family. Whose wife would the woman be in the resurrection? It was a false question because they were inquiring about something in which they didn't believe. Perhaps they were looking for a way to discount the rest of His teaching.

When I became a believer in Yeshua, I found myself drawn to

the way in which He communicated; He was like no one I had ever studied before. But coming upon this situation with the Sadducees really stumped me. Certainly Yeshua was not naïve. Why, then, did He bother to answer this false question put forth by the Sadducees?

Reading over this portion of Matthew, I found my answer in verse 33: "And when the multitudes heard [His explanation], they were astonished at His teaching." It seemed to me that Yeshua's concern was not so much a response to the taunting Sadducees, but for the sake of the multitudes who might be led astray by their false teaching.

When you're witnessing to your Jewish neighbor you, too, might be asked a false question. For example, "If Hitler had believed, could he have gone to heaven?" You could respond in a straightforward manner stating exactly what you believe. Keep in mind that this may be more than a question about your theological beliefs. It may really be designed to find out how you or your "religion" feels about the persecution of Jews.

Using discernment, you could turn the question to the subject of God's judgment, righteousness, and mercy. Express your horror at what Hitler did. Ask your Jewish neighbor if he or she even believes in heaven and hell, and if not, why the question is really being asked.

We must look behind the question in order to discern what is really going on. Perhaps your Jewish neighbor really does care about what happened to Hitler. But it's more likely that he's curious about your beliefs, or is looking for a way to conveniently disengage from your witness.

The truth is, the question is rather absurd. Given the nature of Hitler, and the apparent unrelenting hardening of his heart, it seems beyond comprehension for him to have repented. Truly, it's a question that doesn't deserve an answer. Proverbs 26:4 states, "Do not answer a fool according to his folly, lest you also be like him."

In Yeshua's response to the false question posed to Him, He used the opportunity to preach a little sermon on the resurrection to those within earshot. He gave an answer, but it wasn't the one that the Sadducees had expected. You, too, can use a false question to lead someone closer to the Kingdom of heaven.

## The Testing Question (Matthew 22:34–40 and Mark 12:28–34)

The Pharisees had sent the Herodians to Yeshua. Then the Sadducees had had a go at Him. Next came the scribes, experts in the fine points of Jewish Law. Matthew tells us that their purpose was to test Him.

The scribes were technically conversant in all 613 commandments found in the Torah. The study of these *mitzvot* occupied each of their waking moments. Perhaps they could get Yeshua to answer a question about these God-given standards of behavior. "Teacher," they asked, "which is the great commandment in the Law?"

Perhaps this was the standard test the scribes administered to any professed teacher of the Jewish people. Or perhaps they were setting Yeshua up to give a "wrong" answer.

The logical choice for Yeshua might have been to focus upon the Sabbath, since the keeping of the Sabbath had taken on supreme importance among the Jews of that day. The rules and regulations of Sabbath-keeping had become a favorite topic of discussion. Matthew had already described a conflict that had flared up when Yeshua's disciples were accused of breaking the Sabbath by picking food (Matthew 12:1–8). Perhaps the Pharisees sought to test Yeshua's attitude concerning the Sabbath.

Another of the day's central issues involved *kashrut*—keeping kosher. Jews were restricted in what they could eat. Pork and shrimp were out. Meat could not be eaten together with milk products. To this day there are those trained in *kashrut*, people who earn a living deciding on the fitness of certain products. If you examine the packages of many foods in grocery stores you will notice a "U" in a circle. This means the food has been certified by a rabbi to be kosher. The Pharisees that tested Yeshua might have been interested in His thoughts on these restrictions.

Perhaps they were interested in His thoughts on the issue of circumcision. This sign of the covenant was then and is still a controversial subject in the Jewish community.

Whatever lay behind the original question, Yeshua chose to respond to the test by quoting the *Sh'ma*. *Sh'ma* is Hebrew for "hear." It is the beginning word of the central creed of faith for Jewish people, recited in every synagogue service. Yeshua is quoted as saying this greatest commandment—and the second greatest—in Mark 12:29–31:

> " 'HEAR, O ISRAEL! THE LORD OUR GOD IS ONE LORD; AND YOU SHALL LOVE THE LORD YOUR GOD WITH ALL YOUR HEART, AND WITH ALL YOUR SOUL, AND WITH ALL YOUR MIND, AND WITH ALL YOUR STRENGTH.' The second is this, 'YOU SHALL LOVE YOUR NEIGHBOR AS YOURSELF.' There is no other commandment greater than these."

His audience stood there, amazed. In those two short sentences Yeshua had summarized the Law and the prophets. Ignoring their actual question, He spoke to the heart of the question behind it, namely, "What is most important to God?" He did not get tangled up in the test. He went beyond it. Not only that, but all Jewish people agree that the *Sh'ma* is the greatest statement of their faith. So instead of getting mixed up in disputation over the Law, He affirmed the Law in a very Jewish way. And why wouldn't He? He was a Jew.

You might hear a testing question from your Jewish neighbor. He might ask something that, at first hearing, sounds unimportant to your purpose of teaching him about his Messiah.

One such test question revolves around the issue of the abundance of Christian denominations: "You say there is one Truth," this question begins. "Why then are there dozens of denominations each advocating its own interpretation of the Bible?" The answer to that question would involve a course in Church history. That's not my field nor is it likely to be yours. But at the core it is really a question of whether or not anyone has the right to say there is one Truth. This is the issue that must be tackled. Regarding the question of Truth, you might point out that just because man is unable to agree on Truth does not negate the possibility that there can be one Truth.

Just as Yeshua's answer soared beyond the Pharisees' testing questions, you too will need to resist the particulars and get down to the real issue, the Messiahship of Yeshua.

None of this is meant to suggest that you become impolite or evasive, rather that you communicate in the style Yeshua used. He often answered questions with questions. He avoided answering directly if direct answers could be purposely misconstrued. He wasn't afraid of confronting people with the insincerity of their queries when appropriate. Yeshua was a most effective communicator; He got His message across to His people.

You care about your Jewish neighbor. You want him or her to know the joy of salvation. Be wise as a serpent and harmless as a dove. Discernment will help you know which creature to emulate and when.

Having touched upon the subject of discernment, let's turn to some more actual questions you may face. Most of us who have been involved with sharing the Messiah with the Jewish people come up with the same lists of questions, the same clumps that need clearing. By presenting them here and explaining how the clumps got there in the first place, I hope to help you break through those barriers to belief.

# 13

## Historical Barriers to Belief
*—or—*
*Breaking Through the Confusion*

You saw in Section III that the history, religion, and culture of the Jewish people are intertwined. In the next three chapters, we will study three areas that pose barriers to belief. The three areas are really intertwined, but I have attempted to separate them for the purpose of examination. I call them historical barriers, theological barriers, and personal barriers to belief. Let's begin with the historical barriers.

### "If Jesus was the Messiah, why have so many atrocities been committed in His name?"

As we have seen, Jewish people are acutely aware of the awful deeds that have been done to our people in the name of Jesus. On a lesser scale some of this may have happened in your own neighborhood.

Many Jewish children have been labeled "Christ-killer" by misguided peers. Many a Jewish family has been snubbed by neighbors who attend church on Sunday. Many Jews have been excluded from country clubs simply because they were Jewish. This behavior cannot be justified, but we can try to explain what lies behind it.

First, those who have persecuted Jews or anyone else in the name of Jesus were probably not real believers. And even if a profession of faith had actually been uttered, it is safe to say that they were not true followers of Yeshua. Many people, even today, attend church but have no personal relationship with the Lord. Some go because it is traditional. "My parents went, the neighbors go, my community expects it, so I'll go, too," is not an uncommon attitude (an attitude that often prevails in the synagogue as well, by the way).

It is a good idea immediately to disclaim and disassociate yourself from the past persecutions of Jews when talking of faith with your Jewish neighbor. Express your sorrow that these things have taken place—and your sadness that they have taken place by so-called Christians. Be quick, too, to disassociate these evildoers from Yeshua Himself. Nowhere do we find Him espousing hatred for His own people. Even when He hung on the cross, abandoned by everyone, including His own disciples, He pleaded, "Father, forgive them; for they do not know what they are doing" (Luke 23:34). He died willingly to atone for the sins of all people.

Yeshua taught love. He inspired gentleness. He practiced peace. He encouraged giving. There is no indication anywhere that He would have condoned the violence perpetrated by His so-called followers. Rather, He would have despised it.

Use the opportunity, if confronted with this question, to encourage your Jewish neighbor to read the Sermon on the Mount. It should be evident that persecution of Jews is far from what Yeshua stood for.

### "How can I trust the New Testament? It's anti-Jewish— anti-Semitic!"

Your neighbor may at one time have read some of the New Covenant and come across what he might consider hateful diatribes against the Jewish people. Certain statements from the New Covenant appear to attack some of the Jewish people. In fact, some of these verses have been used to justify anti-Semitic attitudes and behavior.

How do you explain these statements?

First, remind your neighbor that the New Covenant is a Jewish document, written *about* Jews, *by* Jews.

We might look at some of their comments about their fellow Jews in this way. It is not uncommon to criticize one's relatives, particularly within the context of a family gathering. "Cousin Rozzie ought to lose weight" or "It's about time Uncle Harry got a job." But let an outsider say anything about Cousin Rozzie or Uncle Harry, and these relatives will be defended vehemently. Likewise, the New Covenant recorded some statements from Jews about other Jews. That can't be anti-Semitic.

Still, even the most avid antagonist of Yeshua might admit that the harsh things said concerning some of the Jewish people were true. Writings from the time of Yeshua point out that much of the criticism in the New Covenant leveled at some Jews was on target. Corruption had infiltrated the office of the high priest, so much so that it had become a political, rather than religious, office. A sense of self-righteousness prevailed among many of the Pharisees. The *am ha aretz*, the common people, were disdained by the leadership in Israel. Sin was present throughout the land. The New Covenant is not alone in pointing out these problems. But since the *Br'it Chadashah* was used by anti-Semites through the ages to persecute Jews, it is seen as anti-Semitic.

Yeshua's criticism of the hypocritical practices of some of the Jewish people was nothing new. The accusations were no harsher than those of the ancient prophets of Israel. It was Isaiah who penned the following words:

> Alas, sinful nation, people weighed down with iniquity, offspring of evildoers, sons who act corruptly! They have abandoned the Lord, they have despised the Holy One of Israel, they have turned away from Him. . . . The whole head is sick, and the whole heart is faint. From the sole of the foot even to the head there is nothing sound in it.
>
> ISAIAH 1:4–6

No, the words of the *Br'it Chadashah* are not anti-Jewish. Yeshua did not hate His own people. He, like the prophets before Him, hated sin. The statements He made were directed at certain Jews and they concerned particular problems. His words were no harsher than many found in the older Covenant. In all of Scripture, God's purpose in confronting sin was that He could show His steadfast and everlasting love when His people repented.

### "If Jesus is the Messiah, why haven't rabbis believed in Him?"

To begin with you need to know something that may surprise you. Although you'd think that Jewish people would listen carefully to their rabbi, giving this barrier to belief some basis, the truth is that most Jews nowadays are generally not too concerned with what the rabbis believe or teach. There are groups in which the rabbi truly does have the last word. These ultra-Orthodox groups, called *Hassidim,* submit to the authority of their rabbis. It is unlikely that your Jewish neighbor is part of one of these groups, since they generally live together in tightly knit and self-sufficient communities.

So, your Jewish neighbor might be bringing up the question about the rabbis' unbelief in Yeshua as a way of saying, "If our Jewish scholars don't buy into your conclusion that Jesus is the Messiah, then why should I?"

Your response might be that many rabbis *have* believed. Yeshua Himself was called *Rabbi*. Paul, the former Saul of Tarsus, was a noted rabbi. Nicodemus, who came to Yeshua by night, was called a ruler of the Jews and was, most probably, a rabbi. Through the years there have been many rabbis who have believed.

"Then why don't we know about them?" your neighbor might ask. But even as he does, he will already realize the answer to this question. If a rabbi became a believer in Yeshua, he would be immediately defrocked and his name expunged from the rabbinical records. He certainly would not receive publicity in the Jewish community. His credibility would be brought into question. Murmurings concerning his mental state or his commitment to the Jewish people and to the Torah would be heard.

Scripture teaches that eyes of faith are a gift from God. God "has mercy on whom He desires, and He hardens whom He desires" (Romans 9:18). Yeshua preached to the lowly. Even in His day, His message did not appeal to those who considered themselves experts in the ways of God. Paul showed his understanding of God's ways when he wrote that "God has chosen the foolish things of the world to shame the wise, and God has chosen the weak things of the world to shame the things which are strong . . . that no man should boast before God" (1 Corinthians 1:27, 29).

### "We Jews have never proselytized. Why don't you just leave us alone?"

To begin with, it is *not* true historically that Jews have never proselytized. Today, it might be said that Jews don't proselytize, but centuries ago it was not that way.

The very reason God chose Israel was that she would be a light unto the nations, the Gentiles. Throughout Bible history, the Jews are seen as a testimony people, from the Tabernacle to the Messiah. It was always God's intention to use this people to bring glory to Himself and show the world a better way.

Through the ages, the nation of Israel has been a testimony to the existence and love of a living God. Who could read the Scripture accounts of God's wooing His people back from sin and rebellion (the book of Hosea is a moving example) and doubt His commitment to this people? In spite of centuries of dispersion in unfriendly foreign lands and untold persecutions, who can deny that a supernatural force has been protecting the Jewish people?

In the early days of the New Covenant there was much outreach activity on the part of the Jewish people. Finding themselves dispersed throughout the Middle East, they made many converts to Judaism. References in the New Covenant to proselytes and God-fearing Gentiles indicate that the Jewish people were not averse to bringing outsiders into Judaic practices. After all, they were only doing their job, bearing the light of monotheism to the polytheistic pagan nations. The ultimate performance of this role, of course, was by the apostle Paul, an Orthodox Jew who became the bearer of the Good News to the Gentile world.

If we believe what Yeshua said, it behooves believers to be sharing this message with anyone we can find, as Paul said, "to the Jew first and also to the Greek" (Romans 1:16). Call it communicating. Call it proselytizing. Call it missionizing. Does it matter what it's called if the message is true? We are obliged to preach the Gospel.

When Jewish people say, "We don't proselytize," what they are really saying is, "You shouldn't either." The implication is that there is no Truth. That one person's opinion is as good as another's. It is an admission that the Jewish people are a long way from the days of being a light to the nations. But if there *is* a truth, a real, objective truth, then sharing that truth is always appropriate. If your Jewish neighbor were dying of a disease for which you had the cure, the administration of that remedy would certainly be timely and fitting. It would not be considered proselytizing. It would be called caring.

Telling Jews about the Messiah is a far more caring thing to do even than sharing a cure for disease. Spiritual wholeness, having the relationship with God that He intended, is more important than physical well-being.

It is a sad indictment of modern-day Judaism that there is little proselytizing. Perhaps if the Jewish people were convinced of the truth of Judaism as it is observed today, they would find it to be a message compelling them to share. Regardless of this, if *you* know the truth, then you also know that that truth ought to be proclaimed, especially to those people to whom that truth was first revealed.

The statement that "Jews don't proselytize" is merely a modern-day phenomenon, for in the past Jews fulfilled their role as a testimony people. Further, you ought to make it very clear that you are not witnessing so as to "convert" your Jewish neighbor and turn him or her into a Gentile; your only interest is to help your Jewish neighbor meet his or her own Messiah. You have the cure for much more than disease; you have the cure for sin.

Don't be ashamed of your efforts to evangelize. It may cause some friction, but if you have laid the foundation for your relationship, that friendship will withstand this new aspect.

Remember, most of the historical barriers to belief are built upon misunderstanding. If you take the time to talk with and listen to your Jewish neighbor, you might be able to break down some of these barriers and pave the way for communication and witness.

# 14

# Theological Barriers to Belief
## —or—
## *Breaking Through Questions of Doctrine*

Most Jewish people are not theologians. Nor, for that matter, are most believers. But all of us, believers and unbelievers, Jews and non-Jews, wrestle with theological questions of one kind or another. For Jewish people, there are some barriers to belief that we could classify as theological. They center around the Trinity and the Sonship of Yeshua, the virgin birth, substitutionary atonement, the resurrection of the dead, the afterlife, and the apparent "failure" of Yeshua to bring about world peace. Often these barriers to belief are expressed in the same way by different Jewish people. And they are often put in the form of a question.

## "How can you Christians worship three gods? We Jews worship one!"

This misconception is common among Jewish people who don't understand what is meant by the Trinity (or tri-unity). I remember thinking that the holy Trinity was a kind of family: God, the holy Father; the virgin Mary, the holy Mother; and Jesus Christ, the holy Son.

But even when Jewish people understand that the Trinity is really Father, Son, and Holy Spirit, it still sounds suspiciously like three gods. And if this is true, it is tantamount to polytheism, an unbiblical belief anathema to Jews.

A word of friendly advice. Don't fall into the trap of trying to explain the doctrine of the Trinity. If God wanted us to have an easy explanation, He would have provided us with one! Theologians have wrestled with ways to explain the unique nature of God for years. There are explanations, such as the water—liquid, ice, steam— theory. But that and other explanations really seem to fall short. Nothing on this earth is wholly satisfactory to explain the unique nature of the One who created the universe out of nothing. It would be arrogant for us to assume the task of trying to explain His nature, beyond that which He has carefully revealed.

But there is an answer to the accusation "You Christians worship three gods." Reply simply, "No, we don't!" As mentioned in the introduction to this section, Yeshua Himself, quoting the *Sh'ma* (Deuteronomy 6:4), said, "Hear, O Israel! The Lord our God is one Lord" (Mark 12:29). Yeshua was monotheistic!

You can also show that the word translated "one" in the *Sh'ma* is the Hebrew word *echad*. *Echad* is a word that indicates a unique composite unity as in Adam and Eve's becoming "one flesh" (Genesis 2:24). There is another Hebrew word, *yachid*, which is also translated "one" indicating an absolute singular unity, like the number one. But in the *Sh'ma*, the central creed of Jewish faith, the Spirit moved upon Moses in such a way that he chose to write the word *echad*.

So sensitive was this issue that the great rabbi and scholar Maimonides, in his "Thirteen Articles of Faith," took great pains to substitute the word *yachid* for *echad* in his description of God's nature, even to the point of rephrasing the *Sh'ma*. Many feel that this was his attempt to counter the Trinitarian view espoused by the Church. Nonetheless, what Maimonides did was contrary to Tenakh since nowhere is God ever referred to as *Adonai Yachid*.

You could also show some allowance in Tenakh for the concept of composite unity. For instance, the Hebrew Scriptures frequently use plural references for God. The Hebrew word *Elohim*, translated "God," is plural. This is not a great argument, however, because there are some other plausible explanations—for example, the use of the plural to connote royalty, or even used in an editorial sense.

You might also point to some ancient Jewish writings that refer to a "threefold divine manifestation" of God. But it is probable that neither you nor your neighbor has ever curled up with the *Zohar*, a book of Jewish mystical writings.

The simplest way for you to respond to the question of the Trinity, and the ground on which you might feel most comfortable, would be simply to say, "I know why you think that, but really we believers don't worship three gods at all. In fact, we worship the God of Israel—the God of Abraham, Isaac, and Jacob—the same God you worship."

If you feel comfortable getting into Scripture with your Jewish neighbor, there are some specific Bible references that support the plural unity of God.

Isaiah 48:16 reads,

> "Come near to Me, listen to this: from the first I have not spoken in secret, from the time it took place, I was there. And now the Lord God has sent Me, and His Spirit."

This passage—in which God was speaking through the prophet Isaiah—seems to involve three divine Persons: the "Lord God," "Me," and "His Spirit." The "Me" spoken of seems to have the same eternal nature as God Himself, yet is sent by God, along with His Spirit.

There are also references to "the angel of the Lord," who is identified with God. In Genesis 16:7–12 "the angel of the Lord" spoke to Hagar, Sarai's handmaid. Genesis 16:13 states, "Then she called the name of the Lord who spoke to her, 'Thou art a God who sees.' " A similar situation appears in Genesis 22, where "the angel of the Lord" constrained Abraham from slaying his son. These verses clearly identify "the angel of the Lord" with God.

Concerning the Holy Spirit, or the Spirit of God, we read of His presence as far back as Genesis 1:2, where "the Spirit of God was moving over the surface of the waters." We read also in Isaiah 11:2, "The Spirit of the Lord will rest on Him" (the Messiah). There are many other examples as well where "the Spirit of God" performs many of the activities and functions attributed to God.

One last comment on this subject. Occasionally you will hear the related statement, "How can God have a Son?" Granted, the concept of Yeshua's Sonship is a little hard to grasp. Obviously, Yeshua was not a Son in the way in which we are familiar with the term. He wasn't born from God's wife as you might find in Greek mythology. He didn't "grow up in God's home" as our sons do. His Sonship means something entirely different. Let me show you what I mean.

To use the word *son* expresses the idea that one possesses the specific personality and identity of the father. This does not always mean a solely physical bond. For instance, Yeshua renamed James and John *Boanerges,* "Sons of Thunder," giving us a vivid picture of two boisterous men who deserved this fitting nickname (Mark 3:17).

Early in Israel's history God spoke of Israel as "My son, My firstborn" (Exodus 4:22).

In one way we all can be considered sons of God when we claim His Son as our Savior. But Yeshua was different. He was *the* Son of God. He was God's unique Son because He was the incarnation of God Himself.

According to Hebrews 1:3, Yeshua "is the radiance of His glory and the exact representation of His nature." Like the rays from the sun, Yeshua shows us the true essence of all that is God. Now sun rays are not the sun itself, but they are inseparable from it, because without the sun, there would be no rays. Yet we know the rays are distinct because we can see the light in the sky of suns of other solar systems that have long since burned out. What we see are the rays that were generated by those suns thousands of years ago.

Two other passages overwhelmingly support the truth that God has a Son. Psalm 2:7 states: "I will surely tell of the decree of the Lord: He said to Me, 'Thou art My Son, today I have begotten Thee.' " This psalm is referred to by Luke in Acts 13:33.

A second and perhaps even more persuasive passage comes in the form of a riddle from the Tenakh and can even be used that way in your own witnessing. Referring to God, it asks:

Who has ascended into heaven and descended? Who has gathered the wind in His fists? Who has wrapped the waters in His garment? Who has established all the ends of the earth? What is His name or *His Son's name?* Surely you know!

PROVERBS 30:4, EMPHASIS ADDED

All Persons of the tri-unity can be found in the Tenakh. That in itself allows for this seemingly foreign concept to be considered "kosher" for Jewish people. But, once again, explaining it thoroughly is too tall an order for even the best theologian. I suggest when sharing with your Jewish neighbor you simply show that Yeshua's teaching was that God is One, as seen in His quoting of the *Sh'ma.* Further, you might share some of the other verses I have offered to show that the Old Covenant allows for—and even points to—the plural nature of the one true God.

"How can a man be born from a virgin? This is simply not possible!"

Obviously your Jewish neighbor is referring to the miraculous conception of Yeshua. And, interestingly enough, the explanation to this question is one of the easier ones to offer your Jewish neighbor.

The question really goes back to the sovereignty of God. If God can create the heavens and the earth and all that is in them out of nothing, as taught in Tenakh, then creating a person through miraculous means is really no problem. For us it would be impossible. For God, it's no big deal.

Also, consider the fact that it was through miraculous conception that God created the Jewish people. It is no coincidence that the wives of all three patriarchs, Abraham, Isaac, and Jacob, were barren. Genesis 18:11, 25:21, and 29:31 teach us that God opened the wombs of Sarah, Rebekah, and Rachel. Since it was through the divine and miraculous intervention of the almighty God that the Jewish nation was born, it seems entirely consistent that the Redeemer of the Jewish people would also be born through miraculous means.

Couldn't it be true that in these divine acts God was giving us a hint of the future miraculous birth by which the Messiah would come to dwell among us? Remember, your Jewish friend might be operating from an anti-supernatural bias. The miraculous conception of Yeshua would really be no problem for Him who created the heavens and the earth.

"How can you believe in substitutionary atonement? We Jews don't believe that anyone can atone for someone else's sins!"

The statement that Jews don't believe in substitutionary atonement is both true and false. Nowadays, it is true. But in Bible days it was not.

Since the destruction of the Temple and the end of the sacrificial system in 70 C.E., rabbis have tried to offer alternative methods to atone for sin. With the loss of the Temple, the only place for the sacrifice was gone. And without the sacrifice, there was no scriptural way to atone for sin.

Discussions concerning this dilemma appear throughout Jewish writings. "How do we make the reconciliation with God that He requires without His prescribed sacrifice?" the sages asked. Instead of recognizing that God Himself had fulfilled the sacrificial requirement once and for all through the death of Yeshua, the rabbis set out to find another solution.

The answer they developed centered around "works." Performing *mitzvot,* good deeds, they reasoned, must be God's alternative plan for atonement. While there is nothing wrong with performing good deeds, this was never God's plan for atonement lest people get self-satisfied.

Three particular *mitzvot* were offered as solutions for the problem of the missing Temple. First was *t'shuvah* (repentance), then *tsedakah* (charity), and finally *t'filah* (prayer). These activities were the rabbis' alternative program for earning forgiveness. On Yom Kippur, the Day of Atonement, no sacrifice is offered; instead, Jewish people are to practice *t'shuvah, tsedakah,* and *t'filah.*

And so, today, Jewish people report, "We Jews don't believe in substitutionary atonement!" So when you, in your Jewish Gospel message, present the fact that Yeshua died for their sins, they probably won't relate to it. The concept is foreign to most Jewish people.

Jewish people, especially those committed to keeping other Jewish people from being exposed to the Gospel, are sometimes fond of quoting Hosea 6:6, "I desired mercy, and not sacrifice" (KJV). This is a misapplication of the verse. Some may be reacting to what is seen as hypocrisy, where a sinner comes to church on Sunday, is "absolved" of his sins, only to go out the next week to sin again. Any true believer would hardly consider this form of religion to be walking the walk of true Messianic faith.

Those who misapply Hosea 6:6 in an attempt to discount the sacrifice of Yeshua assume that the *Br'it Chadashah,* the New Covenant, doesn't teach that God desires more from His children than the motions of religion. What they fail to see is that Yeshua Himself quotes this very verse as seen in Matthew 9:13.

The question then boils down to this: Do believers teach that all you need to have is a sacrifice and you will be saved? The answer is no! John the Immerser taught, "Repent, for the kingdom of heaven is at hand" (Matthew 3:2). Yeshua, the Messiah, restated this same message at the beginning of His public ministry (Matthew 4:17).

James, in his discussion of faith and works, echoes this very sentiment:

> What use is it, my brethren, if a man says he has faith, but he has no works? Can that faith save him? . . . Even so faith, if it has no works, is dead, being by itself.
>
> JAMES 2:14, 17

James says that we are saved by the kind of faith that results in good works. Otherwise, our faith is stillborn. He is not suggesting that works are required *for* salvation; he is saying that works should result *from* salvation. This is why Yeshua teaches, "You will know them by their fruits" (Matthew 7:20).

Believers ought to have no dispute with the desire of the Jewish people to perform *mitzvot*, good deeds. Indeed, society has prospered because of the worthwhile and noble contributions of Jewish people. *Good deeds, however, do not atone for sin.* For this, God set up a system. This principle of substitution appears clearly in the Torah, as stated before:

> "For the life of the flesh is in the blood, and I have given it to you on the altar to make atonement for your souls; for it is the blood by reason of the life that makes atonement."
>
> LEVITICUS 17:11

Here is stated the life-for-life principle that constitutes the foundation of the Christian, or Messianic, faith. Yeshua died for our sins. He gave His life through the shedding of His blood. He gave it to make atonement for our souls, as Leviticus 17:11 prefigures.

Since most Jews are unfamiliar with the concept of vicarious or substitutionary atonement, you may find this a barrier to belief. Therefore, you'll need to show your Jewish neighbor this essential component of faith, with its foundation in Leviticus and its fulfillment in Yeshua. Isaiah 53 depicts a Jewish person dying for the sins of His people. Daniel 9 describes the Messiah as being "cut off" before the destruction of the Temple. Taken together, these passages compose a pretty good argument for what Yeshua did when He died on the Roman cross on a hill known as Calvary.

**"Why do you Christians believe in the dead coming back to life? We Jews don't believe in the resurrection of the dead."**

If your neighbor postulates that Jewish people don't believe in resurrection, you can contend that resurrection is indeed a Jewish concept. Not only can it be found in the Tenakh, but resurrection was and is taught by religious Jews to this day. What your Jewish neighbor is really saying is, "Most Jews don't believe in the resurrection of the dead." That is true. But here are a few references to resurrection found in the Tenakh:

"And many of those who sleep in the dust of the ground will awake, these [who awake] to everlasting life, but the others [who remain in the grave] to disgrace and everlasting contempt."

DANIEL 12:2

And:

I will ransom them from the power of Sheol; I will redeem them from death.

HOSEA 13:14

As we saw before, the Sadducees, who did *not* believe in resurrection, came to Yeshua ostensibly to question Him about it, underscoring the fact that it was a prevalent doctrine at this time.

Maimonides, the great rabbinical scholar of the 1100s, wrote in his "Thirteen Articles of Faith" Article Thirteen:

I believe with perfect faith in the resurrection of the dead at a time which will please the Creator, blessed be His name, and exalted be His memory for ever and ever.

This was written more than a thousand years after the time of Yeshua.

Clearly, Jews believed in resurrection in the days of Tenakh, in the days of Yeshua, and for hundreds, even thousands of years since. I'm quite confident that if you talk to some Orthodox Jews today, you will find this belief present in their religious thinking. One Orthodox rabbi, Pinchas Lapide, recently wrote that he is convinced that Yeshua Himself was resurrected from the dead. On the back cover of his book *The Resurrection of Jesus: A Jewish Perspective* (Augsburg Publishing House, Minneapolis, 1983), he is quoted as saying, "I accept the resurrection of Easter Sunday not as an invention of the community of disciples, but as a historical event." This man, however, is not ready to confess that Yeshua is the Messiah. Rather, he says He is the Messiah for the Gentiles.

Jews do—or at least did—believe in the resurrection of the dead. This is something you'll need to teach your Jewish friend should you hear the statement, "Jews don't believe in the resurrection of the dead."

**"What makes you believe in an afterlife? We Jews don't believe in heaven and hell."**

Once again this statement really reveals how far popular Judaism has strayed from the once-accepted truths of biblical and Jewish theology. Although there is less emphasis on the afterlife than one finds in most Christian circles, the doctrines of heaven and hell do have strong roots in Jewish thought. In Jewish parlance the terms are *Gan Eden,* literally, "the Garden of Eden," meaning "the world to come," and *Gehenna,* named after a place of garbage-burning.

It was said of Jochanan ben Zakai, mentioned earlier in connection with the development of rabbinic Judaism, that on his deathbed he was fearful for the future. Asked by his disciples why he was crying, he said that he didn't know where he would go when he met his Maker.

Today's most widely held position by those who *do* believe in an afterlife is usually that the quality of one's deeds determines where a person ends up. Each year on Rosh Hashanah, the Jewish New Year, tradition teaches that God opens up His books in heaven. These are considered to be His books of accounts, with debits and credits. Looking things over, God prepares to write your name in one of three places: in the book of the totally righteous, in the book of the totally unrighteous, or in the book of the in-between.

As you might expect, most everyone qualifies for inclusion in the book of the in-between. You are then given ten days, until Yom Kippur, to make amends with those whom you have wronged in the past year, to balance your account. These ten days are called the Days of Awe, *Yomin Noraim,* and when they are over Jewish tradition teaches that your fate is sealed for the next year.

Although heaven and hell are not widely held doctrines, they still do exist in Jewish theology, and though most Jewish people don't buy into the system, still the system is there. If your Jewish friend says that Jews don't believe in these concepts, you can show that it may be true today, but historically it is not.

### "If Jesus was the Messiah, why isn't there peace on earth?"

Today, Jewish people who are truly looking for the Messiah expect Him to bring peace to the earth as is stated in Scripture:

> And He will judge between the nations, and will render decisions for many peoples: and they will hammer their swords into plowshares, and their spears into pruning hooks. Nation will not lift up sword against nation, and never again will they learn war.
>
> ISAIAH 2:4

> And the wolf will dwell with the lamb, and the leopard will lie down with the kid, and the calf and the young lion and the fatling together; and a little boy will lead them. Also the cow and the bear will graze; their young will lie down together; and the lion will eat straw like the ox. And the nursing child will play by the hole of the cobra, and the weaned child will put his hand on the viper's den. They will not hurt or destroy in all My holy mountain, for the earth will be full of the knowledge of the Lord as the waters cover the sea.
>
> ISAIAH 11:6–9

These and other portions of Scripture that talk about world peace someday are often associated with the coming of the Messiah. In past generations Jewish people waxed on about all the wonderful things that would happen "when the Messiah comes." There would be no more poverty, suffering, pain, and certainly no more war.

You can understand, then, that people familiar with the predictions of world peace and universal prosperity have trouble seeing in Yeshua the fulfillment of their expectations. I often hear, "There have been more wars since the time of Jesus than in all the history before Him!" This is undoubtedly true. And it's a sad commentary on the supposedly enlightened world in which we live, especially a world with so many believers. This, too, however, is described in the Word of God:

> And as He was sitting on the Mount of Olives, the disciples came to Him privately, saying, "Tell us, when will these things be, and what will be the sign of Your coming, and of the end of the age?" And Jesus answered and said to them, "See to it that no one misleads you. For many will come in My name, saying, 'I am the Christ [Messiah],' and will mislead many. And you will be hearing of wars and rumors of wars; see that you are not frightened, for those things must take place, but that is not yet the end. For nation will rise against nation, and kingdom against kingdom, and in various places there will be famines and earthquakes."
>
> MATTHEW 24:3–7

This is not a comforting description. But it's something we can readily identify around us. These words were spoken by the Messiah, not preaching peace and prosperity, but describing a world to which He would one day return. With that return He will bring the peaceful reign that Jewish people expect from the Messiah.

> And I saw a new heaven and a new earth; for the first heaven and the first earth passed away, and there is no longer any sea. And I saw the holy city, new Jerusalem, coming down out of heaven from God, made ready as a bride adorned for her husband. And I heard a loud voice from the throne, saying, "Behold, the tabernacle of God is among men, and He shall dwell among them, and they shall be His people, and God Himself shall be among them, and He shall wipe away every tear from their eyes; and there shall no longer be any death; there shall no longer be any mourning, or crying, or pain; the first things have passed away."
>
> REVELATION 21:1–4

To deal with the difficulty of the Messiah's having come, yet not establishing world peace, you must show that His work is not finished. Yeshua Himself told His followers that there will not only be more and more wars, but famines, earthquakes, and bad news in the world. The good news is that there will be an end to all the misery with the coming of the "new Jerusalem," when Yeshua reigns as King over the entire earth. But you need to point out that no one enters the Kingdom without establishing peace with God, as it is written: "So, since we have come to be considered righteous by

God because of our trust, let us continue to have *shalom* with God through our Lord, Yeshua, the Messiah" (Romans 5:1, JNT).

Now that you are better equipped to break through the theological barriers, let's turn to some of the personal barriers to belief you might face as you share the Gospel with your Jewish neighbor.

# 15

## Personal Barriers to Belief
### —or—
### *Breaking Through Individual Objections to Faith*

"**W**hy do I need someone to atone for my sins? I'm a good person!"

None of us finds it easy to face our sins. Most of us have a highly developed system of what psychologists call defense mechanisms. Yet the Bible teaches that we all sin and come short of the glory of God.

Your Jewish neighbor may actually be one of the finest, most decent people you know. Jews are renowned for their concern for the downtrodden, care for the sick, and commitment to civil justice. They often adhere to high standards of behavior and, as a group, expect themselves to be morally superior to others around them. Remember, the Jewish people were originally intended to set an example for the rest of the nations. Even when a Jew does not believe in God, there often exists a leftover sense of responsibility to uphold the high standards of moral conduct.

Assuming that your Jewish neighbor is a "good person," you need to communicate that God is not dealing merely with outward manifestations of kindness and goodness. He looks on the heart and judges sin. He knows what is going on deep down inside.

The rabbis describe two forces that they see operating within a person: the *yetzer ha tov,* the good inclination, and the *yetzer ha ra,* the evil inclination. They say these inclinations impact moral choice. The apostle Paul described his struggle as a continual warring between the flesh and the spirit. He summed it up in words with which we all can readily identify, "For the good that I wish, I do not do; but I practice the very evil that I do not wish" (Romans 7:19). In other words, he could not live up to the high standard of God's righteousness.

Most people, although hesitant to admit that they are sinners, nevertheless sense that both Paul's statement and the rabbinical concept ring with truth. Man has a nature to sin. That nature is what Yeshua came to deal with. He came to atone for our sins and, by the Holy Spirit of God, do away with anything that goes against the will of God.

Your Jewish neighbor needs to feel assured of a few things: that you value his or her friendship; that you appreciate the good things he or she does; and that you believe God is also glad for those good deeds.

But your Jewish neighbor also needs to understand what Isaiah wrote concerning himself and his people: "All of us have become like one who is unclean, and all our righteous deeds are like a filthy garment" (Isaiah 64:6). He needs to hear what King David had to say: "There is no one who does good, not even one" (Psalm 14:3). He needs to recognize that Abraham sinned (Genesis 12:10–20); that Moses sinned (Numbers 20:7–13); that even the beloved David sinned (2 Samuel 11:1–12:12).

Your Jewish neighbor must become aware of the truth that any sin, external or internal, has its consequences. That sin is more a matter of the heart than of the hand. That there is an eternal, spiritual consequence to this sin that affects him and God.

> But your iniquities have made a separation between you and your God, and your sins have hid His face from you, so that He does not hear.
>
> ISAIAH 59:2

As good as your Jewish neighbor is, surely he recognizes that he has encountered an evil inclination, a fleshly thought, a secret sin. In God's eyes, covert sins count as much as overt ones.

One Saturday evening while shopping at a mall I had an opportunity to share the message of the Messiah with some Jewish people. After I explained why the Messiah had to die, they smiled patiently and objected, "But we're good people; we don't need anyone to make atonement for us."

"Do you obey God's laws?" I asked them.

"Certainly!" came the reply.

"What did you do today?" I asked. Judging from the number of bags they were carrying, it looked as if they had spent a good part of the day shopping.

They answered, "We were here at the mall."

"So how is it that you are not obeying the fourth commandment?"

They weren't sure which the fourth commandment was. I reminded them that it instructed us to keep the Sabbath Day holy. Obviously they were not observing it there at the mall.

They began to become aware that they were relying on their own standard for goodness and righteousness. In essence, they had made up their own religion. Many Jewish people will sum up their religious conviction by saying, "I don't do anything that would hurt anyone else." At the same time, though, they don't keep the ways of God.

When He was asked what the greatest commandment was, Yeshua said it was to love God. To love God means to obey Him and seek to please Him. This is where many of us fall short. Yes, we might do good things. But, too often, we fail to love God *first*.

My Jewish people have done their share of good things. This is great! But doing good deeds in an unbelieving context can lead to self-righteousness and turning away from God. It is the nature of humankind. And it was for this very reason that God provided a way to reconcile with Him. Yeshua is that way.

## "Don't you know if I believe in Yeshua, I won't be Jewish anymore?"

This objection always gets to me. It shows just how far Messianic faith has gotten from its Jewish roots.

Most believers have gotten so far from the Jewish roots of their faith, they don't even know they have any. The Church today feels about as Jewish as ham and cheese on white bread with mayonnaise.

What am I saying? For nineteen hundred years, most followers of Yeshua have been Gentile with little reference to the Jewish beginnings of their faith. But it wasn't always like this.

If you recall in the debate of Acts 15, the question concerning the Jerusalem Council revolved around whether or not Gentiles could be saved without first submitting to Jewish Law. Since nearly all the early believers were Jewish, they were not sure how to instruct the non-Jews who also followed the Jewish Messiah.

Certain Jews—particularly among the Pharisees who believed in Yeshua—felt it was "necessary to circumcise the non-Jews, and to direct them to observe the Law of Moses" (Acts 15:5). After much debate, Peter stood and said,

> "God, who knows the heart, bore witness to [the Gentiles], giving them the Holy Spirit, just as He also did to us; and He made no distinction between us and them, cleansing their hearts by faith. Now therefore why do you put God to the test by placing upon the neck of the disciples a yoke which neither our fathers nor we have been able to bear? But we believe that we are saved through the grace of the Lord Jesus, in the same way as they also are."
>
> ACTS 15:8–11

Finally the Council agreed to follow James' suggestion to write the Gentiles at Antioch to "abstain from things contaminated by idols and from fornication and from what is strangled and from blood" (verse 20). The letter was delivered in person by Paul and Barnabas and we read that the church rejoiced because of its encouragement.

Perhaps because the Council did not impose Jewish traditions that might have been stumblingblocks for the Gentiles, or perhaps because the Jewish believers themselves, through the force of persecution, joined in worship with the growing numbers of Gentiles, or perhaps for any number of reasons, the "Jewishness" of Christianity greatly diminished. In relatively few years, what had started out as a Jewish sect became a predominantly Gentile religion.

Nowadays, a new Jewish believer goes through an unmistakable identity crisis. I can still remember lying on my bed the night I invited Yeshua into my life. I was afraid to go to sleep for fear that I might awaken as a Gentile. It wasn't that I was anti-Gentile. Some of my best friends were Gentiles.

I just felt determined to maintain my Jewish identity. For the first time in my life, I understood that God had a special plan for the Jewish people. He had made me a Jew. Still, that night I was fearful that belief in Yeshua might put pressure on me to abandon my heritage. After all, most believers I had met were Gentiles.

But the next morning I awoke craving a bagel, lox, and cream cheese sandwich. Boy, was I relieved!

Actually, I knew in my head I was still a Jew and that nothing would ever change that fact. Believing in Yeshua might have made me an unusual Jew, but a Jew, nonetheless. Being Jewish is a matter of birth, not choice (except for those who convert to Judaism). I was born a Jew and I'll die a Jew. But thanks be to God, when I die as a Jew, I will be in heaven because of the work of another Jew, Yeshua of Nazareth.

If your Jewish neighbor wonders whether or not he will remain a Jew after accepting Yeshua, assure him that he will. There have been other Jews claiming to be the Messiah. They all had their followers. Bar Kokhba, the hero who died in the Roman revolt, had many. Did his devotees cease to be Jews because they followed him? Of course not. And no rabbi today believes Bar Kokhba was the Messiah.

Shabbetai Zvi proclaimed himself to be the Messiah in the 1600s. He had quite a following in Europe. But when he ran into some trouble he converted to Islam. Obviously, not the Messiah.

Others who made Messianic claims had disciples who followed them and adhered to their teaching. Nowhere is there any hint that the Jewish community cut them off saying that they were no longer Jews. This only happens when Jews choose to follow Yeshua. But faith in Him does not cause a person to stop being Jewish no matter what the Jewish community or the rabbis say. That identity was a sovereign work of almighty God. No modern rabbi or Jewish leader can change that.

Many rabbis today take the position that a Jew who accepts Jesus is still a Jew, albeit a wayward Jew. The funeral ceremonies Jewish families once held to mourn a loved one who accepted Yeshua do not often take place anymore. This is due, in part, to the strong stand taken nowadays by Jewish believers. We are now more committed to identifying as Jews, as well as followers of the Messiah Yeshua.

In response, the Jewish community senses that Jewish believers in Yeshua are better Jews than they were before. Now they regularly worship the God of Abraham, Isaac, and Jacob. Now they show a stronger commitment to Israel and her survival, based on belief in the Word of God. Many are even moving there.

Ask your Jewish friend if a Jew who practices transcendental meditation is still Jewish. Ask your Jewish friend if a Jew who is an atheist is still Jewish. Ask your Jewish friend if a Jew who practices yoga is still Jewish. Most likely, the answer will be yes! Then ask why following a Jew who taught Torah and led Jews and Gentiles into a personal relationship with the God of Abraham, Isaac, and Jacob makes one a non-Jew?

To accept Yeshua as Messiah, Savior, and King does not make a Gentile out of a Jew. In fact, Yeshua will make your neighbor a fulfilled Jew!

### "Do you know what will happen in my family if I accept Yeshua as the Messiah and Savior!"

As we just discussed, there was once a time when Jews who accepted Yeshua found themselves unwillingly cut off from their families and friends. It wasn't unusual for the relatives to "sit *shiva*" (mourning for the dead, as we discussed before) for the wayward son or daughter who professed faith in Yeshua. But, thank the Lord, times have changed.

Although it can still be quite upsetting for a family when one among them becomes a believer in Yeshua, it is not as threatening as it once was. In days gone by when a Jewish believer joined a church, he often lost any sense of his Jewish identity. It no longer seemed important to marry another Jew, maintain a Jewish lifestyle, and enjoy the culture of the Jewish people. Indeed, there were so few Jewish believers that such a priority was impractical. It was no longer compelling to visit Israel. It was no longer important to support the causes championed by the Jewish community. Jewish believers were in the same boat as many of the Jewish believers who assimilated in the first century after the separation from the Jewish community began.

Since Jews are in a minority to begin with, to lose even one is seen as a threat to the very existence of the Jewish people. Therefore, when the life of a new Jewish believer began to revolve around the fellowship of his church, the ignoring of the Jewish community made it seem as if he had left his people. And in many ways, indeed he had.

Nowadays, when a Jew becomes a believer, he can maintain his identity and commitment to his Jewish family, friends, and community. One of the reasons for this has been the growth of the Messianic congregational movement.

Over the past decade, hundreds of such congregations have sprung up all over the world. These congregations usually consist of a mixture of Jews and Gentiles who want to worship God in a Jewish way.

The music sounds like other Jewish music. The liturgy contains scripturally appropriate portions from the Jewish prayer books. The holiday celebrations focus on traditional worship enhanced by full Messianic meaning.

For example, Yom Kippur is observed with certain traditions but always with the recognition that Yeshua has made the final atonement for all sin. Passover is observed acknowledging the full impact of the Messiah, our Passover, as Paul referred to Him in 1 Corinthians 5:7.

Many non-Jews enjoy this kind of worship and feel an affinity to the Jewish people and their traditions and customs. There is no "barrier of the dividing wall" as there was in the Temple, separating Jews from Gentiles. Instead Jews and Gentiles worship the one true God together.

Becoming aware of this movement may help you to place your Jewish friend in a worship environment that might help him or her feel at home. *Contextualization* has become a buzz word in mission schools. Missionaries have grown acutely aware of how necessary it is to place the fewest number of stumblingblocks in the path of someone accepting the Gospel message. The Messianic congregation is the height of contextualization for Jewish believers.

Understand that if your Jewish friend accepts Yeshua, there might be some negative reaction from family and friends. This is to be expected. But usually after a short time of adjustment acceptance of his or her new faith will follow. There are people all over the country who can introduce your Jewish neighbor to other Jewish believers who can empathize with what he or she might be experiencing. I'll be sharing contact information later.

Happily, there is today a great openness in the Jewish commu-

nity to the person of Yeshua. Never before in history have so many
Jewish scholars considered Him a credible Jew. Books are released
regularly that discuss Jesus as a great Jewish leader. We even have
a tract called "The Most Famous Jew of All" in which we quote
other famous Jews and the nice things they had to say about Yeshua.
This is a great day for sharing the Good News with Jewish people.

### "Where was God when the 6,000,000 died?"

This probing question does not relate directly to Yeshua, but
rather reflects a relationship, or a nonrelationship, with God. For
many Jews who lived through the Holocaust, belief in a caring,
involved God has become next to impossible. We might have
discussed this question under historical barriers to belief. But
because of the personal impact the Holocaust had on Jewish people,
it fits better into this section.

If God is almighty and cares for His people, they reason, how
could He let the Nazis kill one-third of His chosen people? As you
may expect, this is a very sensitive subject. Frankly, I don't know if
anyone has the answer to this dilemma. While it's certainly true that
after the Holocaust the nation of Israel was reborn, and that this
rebirth was part of God's end-time plan, to throw this out as a
justification for the Holocaust may seem insensitive.

Some say that God promised protection to the Jewish people
only when they were living in the land of Israel. Foretold in
Scripture were dangers and disasters if the Jews were to be expelled
from the land, something that finally happened in 135 C.E. But
again, to point this out to a Jewish person may sound cold and cruel.

Often we hear, "God has given man freedom of choice. He won't
simply step in every time things don't go the way He would desire."
But does that truth ease the pain of having lost a husband or wife,
parent or child, in the Holocaust? No, it doesn't. It's too philo-
sophical.

Perhaps better than trying to answer, "Where was God when the
6,000,000 died?" you might instead try expressing the broken heart
of God when any of His people suffer. I don't think anyone has
adequately explained how 6,000,000 of God's chosen people could
be allowed to suffer and die as they did.

One thing is certain, though. Like all parents, God must have suffered, too. My father used to tell me that when he had to punish me it hurt him worse than it hurt me. I never believed that. It was my "tush" that was red. I couldn't figure it out. Until I became a father. Now I understand. I must assume that God's suffering exceeded that of His people. He is our heavenly Father.

There's no easy way to break through this barrier to belief. Sympathize with your Jewish neighbor. Empathize if you can. It is possible that he or she lost relatives during that dark day in Jewish history. Your understanding might help undo a little of the hurt that is keeping your friend from faith in God.

You now have a pretty good idea of what personal barriers to belief may keep your Jewish neighbor from faith. These clumps, along with the theological and historical clumps, really inhibit the birth of the Gospel seed in many Jewish hearts. They also keep the seed from sprouting and taking root.

But equipped with the right tools and committed to putting in time and patience, you can clear the clumps away. You *can* break through the barriers to belief. You can overcome Jewish objections to trusting in Yeshua. Prepare yourself as best you can and leave the rest up to God. Through your loving witness, Jewish people you know might discover that they are really part of the remnant.

Our last chapter will describe an actual witnessing event. It will serve to summarize much of the material you've already learned and make the point in a fresh way. You've read about this "completion" before. It's the story of the woman at the well.

# 16

## Putting It All Together
*—or—*
*Dropping Your Line for the Lord*

It's not enough to understand the "Gentile Great Commission." It's not enough to know how to sensitize your language. It's not even enough to develop a deeper understanding of your Jewish neighbor or co-worker. And finding out how to break down barriers is again only part of the process. We need to put it all together.

At the beginning of this book, I shared the story of my first fishing expedition, focusing on the fact that Yeshua said He'd make His disciples "fishers of men." That was His promise to those who wished to follow Him, and although it is 2,000 years later, we, too, are His followers. Now, as before, He wants us to be fishers of men.

By example Yeshua gave us wonderful instruction in the art of fishing. The Gospel of John recounts the story simply and effectively. It concerns the Messiah and a woman He met at a well. This transaction is a classic example of persuasive communication—an effective witness.

This seems like an appropriate time to summarize a thought that I've tried to weave through this book. If you remember only one thing, I hope it is this: that witnessing is nothing more than communicating effectively the Good News of Yeshua, the Messiah—that He came and died to atone for our sins. You might forget much that I've shared, but if you remember that witnessing to Jewish people is communicating effectively the truth that their own Messiah has come, you have learned a lot.

Yeshua's whole purpose on this earth was to seek and save the lost. Although most of His ministry was directed toward His own people, He surely had a burden for non-Jews. His Father sent Him to die for their sins, too. They, too, needed a savior. They needed to receive the gift of eternal life.

The woman at the well was not Jewish. She was a Samaritan, part of a people who developed in the Northern Kingdom of Israel under Jereboam after the separation from the Southern Kingdom of Judah.

Samaritans were a mixed race with pagan roots, descended from Jews who had intermarried. Keeping many of the same practices of their brethren in Judah, they revered the Torah, claiming to have a version even older than that of the Jews. They traced their genealogy back to Jacob. They rejected the rest of the Tenakh and developed their own religion, similar to Judaism. In general the Samaritans were despised by the Jews.

In the fourth chapter of John, Yeshua, a Jew, was witnessing to a Samaritan woman, a half-Jew. Let's now observe Yeshua in this witnessing encounter. I find it an encouragement to witness.

## Be Willing

Without question, being willing to witness is the first prerequisite in any kind of evangelism. Perhaps it seems like an obvious statement, but you have taken that first step by reading a book like this. You have shown your desire to serve the Lord by bringing the Gospel to your Jewish neighbor. But you may still need to overcome certain hurdles to continue on your way. Yeshua's example is helpful:

> And He had to pass through Samaria. So He came to a city of Samaria, called Sychar, near the parcel of ground that Jacob gave to his son Joseph; and Jacob's well was there. Jesus therefore, being wearied from His journey, was sitting thus by the well. It was about the sixth hour.
>
> JOHN 4:4–6

Because of His desire to let the Samaritans know that the Savior had arrived, He overcame the hurdles that could have stood in the way of His ministry. He could have offered physical, religious, and social excuses for avoiding the encounter.

In His humanity, Yeshua was tired. He was "wearied from His journey." We find out later that He was thirsty and hungry. He knew what would happen if He asked this woman to get Him a drink, that His request would lead to all kinds of questions. It might even have caused Him less strain simply to get the drink Himself. Yeshua could have thought, "I'm too tired. I need to take care of my physical needs before I can minister to someone else." But He was willing to witness.

A "religious" reason for Him to avoid getting involved was that she was a Samaritan. She herself knew that "Jews [had] no dealings with Samaritans" (John 4:9). Not only did Jews avoid Samaritans, but Orthodox Jews did not (and still do not) converse publicly with women other than their wives.

His social excuse would have been that this was not the kind of woman with whom the Messiah should be seen. She had had five husbands, and the one with whom she was now living was not even her husband (John 4:18). But Yeshua's willingness to witness overcame all of the obstacles.

Will there be any hurdles to overcome to witness to your Jewish neighbor or friend? Will there be practical physical hurdles such as your own busy schedule or the potential loss of business? Will there be religious hurdles such as little experience with Jewish people? Will there be social hurdles such as the discomfort that comes with finding yourself at social events or holiday celebrations that are culturally unusual?

Those obstacles can be overcome in the interest of your witness. Begin with prayer. Pray that you will have the holy boldness to present the Messiah in a clear, forthright way. Pray that your Jewish friend will be willing to listen to you. Pray that the way will be made clear before you, that all the barriers, obstacles, and hurdles might be cleared away, or at least smoothed down a little.

Once you've made up your mind to witness, once you've said you are willing, talk to God about His beloved creature who is your neighbor, your co-worker, your friend. It is God who placed you in the position to witness to the saving gift of the Messiah. Surely, He will help you with your witness . . . if you are willing.

## Create Interest

Imagine how surprised the Samaritan woman was when that Jewish man named Yeshua spoke to her! "How is it that You, being a Jew, ask me for a drink since I am a Samaritan woman?" (John 4:9). She knew very well that Jews and Samaritans didn't get along, didn't even converse. Her interest was piqued.

This is an example of what social psychologists call cognitive dissonance: two conflicting thoughts, concepts, or ideas being placed together. This well-known principle of communication is the subject of many studies.

As I am writing, my younger daughter, Shira, is creating dissonance. She thinks she is playing the piano. Pounding the keys is more like it! Earlier today, my older daughter, Rebecca, was playing the piano. Rebecca takes piano lessons. Shira is younger and hasn't yet begun to study an instrument.

Rebecca's playing did not attract my attention other than to notice that she is playing better and better. She was hitting most of her notes. But what Shira is doing is very disturbing. I can't help but notice it. Dissonance demands attention!

In music dissonance is defined as a simultaneous combination of tones in a state of unrest and needing completion. It is an effective tool in music if used properly. But it can also make for some pretty nasty sounds. One thing is certain, when those dissonant sounds are produced, we notice.

Yeshua, addressing the woman at the well, caused her to experience cognitive dissonance. Here was a Jewish man speaking to her, a Samaritan woman. That wasn't supposed to happen. A naturally talkative and curious person, the woman immediately became puzzled and challenged Yeshua. Of course, He knew she would.

From 1974 to 1980 I served with the Jewish mission Jews for Jesus. That mission succeeds in attracting more media attention than all other Jewish missions combined. People tend to think that all Jewish missions and all Jewish believers are part of the Jews for Jesus organization. It seems as though it is the one group they keep hearing about, even though there are other effective ministries being conducted in America that have been around since before the turn of the century, like Chosen People Ministries (formerly the American Board of Missions to the Jews) and the American Messianic Fellowship.

I am certain that part of the reason Jews for Jesus attracts so much attention is its name. Nowadays "Jews" and "Jesus" are generally not spoken in the same sentence. The cognitive dissonance that comes from the name *Jews for Jesus* arouses the interest of both the Church and the Jewish community.

In your witness to your Jewish friend, you will need to arouse some interest in the Gospel. That's your second step. The way Yeshua did it was to do something out of the ordinary. Dissonance arouses interest. Perhaps you wear a cross. I've already shown how the symbol of the cross can be an affront to Jews. But if your Jewish friend sees you wear a Star of David, that might really arouse interest. Asked why you are wearing it, you can respond by saying something like this: "Because Yeshua, the Messiah, was a descendant of King David." Some believers even wear a Star of David with a cross in the middle of it. Talk about arousing interest!

You might ask your Jewish friend if you could attend synagogue sometime with his or her family. Surely that would raise a question or two. If you are asked why, you might say, "Because I'm interested in seeing the kind of service that Yeshua went to. I know He didn't go to church."

There are lines of special holiday greeting cards that believers can send to Jewish people to show appreciation and arouse interest. Even adding a personal thought to a standard greeting card for Christian or Jewish holidays can be a way of making that connection. For example, in December, you might send a holiday card to your Jewish friend, saying something like, "I thank God for the Jewish people through whom God brought the Messiah and Savior. Merry Messiahmas!"

You can think of other methods to arouse your neighbor's interest, but let me caution you not to contrive a situation. As I used to explain to my communications classes, someone might arrest attention by firing a rifle before beginning to speak. But unless the message was about hunting or gun control or something else gun-related, the rifle shot would be seen as contrived and would ultimately hurt the speaker's credibility.

I urge you to consider pertinent ways to arouse the interest of your Jewish friend. Without first getting your neighbor's attention, no amount of persuasion will succeed.

## Be Timely

Politicians are the subject of much discussion in America. Whether or not a particular politician can get legislation passed, balance budgets, or create positive social change, most likely he or she can communicate. This natural ability to persuade, this aptitude for getting elected term after term, comes from having a knack for addressing the concerns of their constituency. They talk about timely topics, the concerns that matter most. If drug dealers stalk the community, politicians raise their voices in outrage. If pollution is poisoning a river, it will appear on a politician's agenda. The planks of a politician's platform are usually the pertinent affairs of the day. Why? Because timeliness is an essential component of good communication.

Yeshua demonstrated this in His discussion with the woman at the well. She asked Him a question about a Jew talking to a Samaritan and received a timely answer:

> Jesus answered and said to her, "If you knew the gift of God, and who it is who says to you, 'Give Me a drink,' you would have asked Him, and He would have given you living water."
> She said to Him, "Sir, You have nothing to draw with and the well is deep; where then do You get that living water? You are not greater than our father Jacob, are You, who gave us the well, and drank of it himself, and his sons, and his cattle?"
> JOHN 4:10–12

His was not the answer the Samaritan woman had anticipated. She had inquired about interreligious relations, Jews and Samaritans, not water. But in His witness, Yeshua's plan was to get her off of one track and onto another. He planned to move onto spiritual issues in a timely way.

Yeshua had found the woman at a well, not in a store or out in a field. She was there for only one reason—to draw water. What more timely reference could Yeshua have chosen? Living water. Not only did a timely topic increase her interest, it also led to a spiritual dialogue as we shall discover. You may recall that in our earlier chapter about discernment we learned that Yeshua sometimes chose not to answer a question directly. In drawing the woman onto the subject of water, and then living water, Yeshua could not have chosen a better way to respond to her question about Jewish-Samaritan relations.

About ten years ago, Steffi and I were in New Orleans scheduled to minister in a number of churches with a team of musicians. Suddenly it hit us that the Super Bowl was soon to take place in that very city! In a matter of hours we had written a Gospel tract using the theme of the Super Bowl to attract the attention of the thousands of fans in town for the big event. We easily distributed thousands of pamphlets to the receptive crowds. Because the tracts were so timely, folks could hardly wait to get their hands on them! Perhaps they were not as well-written or elaborately presented as some of the tracts you can get in your local Christian bookstore, but the timeliness of the Super Bowl connection went a long way toward spreading the Gospel message.

How can you be timely with your presentation of the Gospel to your Jewish neighbor or friend? To begin with, you can learn through conversation what is on his or her mind. Obviously, football was on the minds of those in New Orleans that January weekend. The situation provided us with a convenient context in which to present the Gospel. Your Jewish neighbor most likely has many things on his or her mind. Try to figure out what these might be and see if you can guide your communication toward these things.

Suppose the newspaper reports a major occurrence in Israel. It seems that major events occur there almost daily. As we have said, most American Jews follow news of the Middle East with concern. Why not bring up the news item as an opportunity to discuss what the Bible says about Israel?

Earlier I mentioned a relative of mine to whom I have been witnessing. The opportunity arose originally when she expressed to me serious reservations concerning the way world opinion seems to be turning against Israel. I was able to get into the Bible (specifically Zechariah 12 and 14) because of the timeliness of what the Bible has to say about Israel.

Consider what would have happened if I tried to approach her by announcing, "Say, why don't we look into the Bible and study about the Messiah!" Most likely, she would have declined politely.

Israel is generally a timely topic to discuss with your Jewish neighbor. But it is not the only one. The newspaper is full of exciting issues that can lead into Bible discussion. I assure you that if you are willing to witness, pray for God's guidance, seek to arouse interest, you will find many timely topics to discuss.

## Speak to Needs

When you attract people's interest and discuss timely topics with them you may well be relating to their needs. By showing how your message can meet these needs, they will be more inclined to hear you out.

Yeshua demonstrated this perfectly. Picture Him sitting by Jacob's well. Picture the Samaritan woman approaching Him, a water pitcher on each of her shoulders. Feel the hot Israeli sun beating down upon her. It was the sixth hour—noon.

After arousing her interest (by simply talking to her) and bringing up a timely topic (living water), Yeshua moved the conversation to a deeper level:

> Jesus answered and said to her, "Everyone who drinks of this water shall thirst again; but whoever drinks of the water that I shall give him shall never thirst; but the water that I shall give him shall become in him a well of water springing up to eternal life."
>
> JOHN 4:13–14

Obviously, Yeshua wasn't talking about $H_2O$. He was referring to a relationship with God. Jeremiah also used the expression *living water:*

> "For My people have committed two evils: They have forsaken Me, the fountain of living waters, to hew for themselves cisterns, broken cisterns, that can hold no water."
>
> JEREMIAH 2:13

God was the living water. Yeshua was saying that knowing God provided permanent refreshment.

We have all experienced the pleasure of drinking a tall glass of water on a particularly scorching day. There are few things in life that make us feel so good. If we are perspired, if we have become parched, that water offers intense pleasure. Drawing near to God offers similar satisfaction for our spiritual thirst.

Yeshua wanted the Samaritan lady to know God; He wished that she would experience the joy of drinking from the springs of salvation. But He knew He had to lead her to this experience. He could have said as He did later in the Gospel of John, "I am the light of the world," but she wasn't looking for a candle. He could have replied, "I am the bread of life," but she wasn't on a picnic. Instead, He spoke about something relevant to her current need. He found her at a well, and spoke to her about water that would cause her never to thirst again.

We see that Yeshua was beginning to get onto spiritual subjects. He spoke about "eternal life" (verse 14), but the Samaritan woman did not get His point. Her response was, "Sir, give me this water, so I will not be thirsty, nor come all the way here to draw" (verse 15).

She had no idea what Yeshua was talking about, and yet somehow she wanted what He was offering. Tired of traipsing back and forth to this well everyday in the hot Israeli sun to get a few pitchers of water, she had a real need. Although Yeshua was interested in her deeper need, He decided to address her in the context of her present need.

We, as His disciples, ought to model ourselves after our Master. If we seek the kind of spirituality evidenced by Yeshua, if we look for ways to be like Him, let us share with people as He did—with relevance, observing people's circumstances and using them as the context for our communications, dealing with people's needs.

It might sound manipulative, but it's not. It is effective. Good communicators always attempt to understand the needs of those with whom they are communicating. Communication ethics require you not to misuse your knowledge, and that your interest be sincere. Surely the One who gave His life for the sin of the world is our greatest example of sincere interest in others.

If someone you knew were about to drive off a cliff, naturally you'd try to warn him or her. Well, unless your Jewish friends have eternal life, they are headed toward that cliff. It is imperative that your witness speak to their needs.

In *Motivation and Personality* (Harper & Row, New York, 1954), the famous humanistic psychologist Abraham Maslow described what he called a hierarchy of people's needs. He reduced mankind's needs into five basic categories: physiology, safety, belongingness, esteem, and self-actualization. Maslow concluded that each level of need must be satisfied before a person can move on to the next level.

Although Maslow would probably not define his message in scriptural terms, still I like his structure because it seems to move, in biblical language, from the flesh to the spirit. A good communicator must know the level on which he must speak in order to deliver his message successfully. A missionary to the down and out is not going to begin ministering by bringing up the subject of eternal life. If the person he's talking to is starving, the missionary must first see to it that he is fed. That, of course, is the approach taken by many inner-city rescue missions.

But, as a general rule, especially in America, there are not that many hungry Jews. Except for a minority of older people who live in pockets of urban poverty, Jewish people today can be found in the middle class or better. So if the person you want to witness to is physiologically satisfied—fed, rested, warm—then you must discover the level of his greatest need. Perhaps he does not feel safe or secure. Perhaps he doesn't feel loved. Maybe circumstances have denied him self-esteem. According to Maslow, all these must be dealt with before the person can become self-actualized. A self-actualized person is one who is living at his own maximum potential. This person is more altruistic. He might be concerned with spiritual things. Until a person's first four needs are satisfied, it is unlikely that he or she will seek to satisfy this higher need.

When we witness we do well to understand the needs of those with whom we share. Although Jewish people are not generally hungry or ill-housed, still there are many who feel a need for safety or security, particularly because of anti-Semitism and anti-Israel attitudes. Also, you'll often find a need for belongingness. Your offer of friendship and fellowship as well as a commitment to the Jewish people and the land of Israel may speak to some of those safety and belongingness needs. In other words, be a friend.

Self-esteem, according to Maslow, is one of man's higher needs. Self-esteem causes a person to feel good about himself. The knowledge that the God who created the universe accepts us even while we are still sinners (Romans 5:8) can give us self-esteem. Jewish people tend to be goal-oriented; years of rabbinical Jewish theology have taught that good works determine our destiny. *Mitzvot,* good deeds, give that person self-esteem. "What can we do?" is usually considered even more important than "What do we believe?"

I remember listening once when the members of my family were discussing the difference between Judaism (as it is practiced today) and Christianity (as they understood it). Their comment will help you understand what I mean when I say that Judaism is works-oriented. "Christians," they alleged, "are concerned about afterlife; Jews are concerned with the here-and-now."

Because of the heavy emphasis on performance, Jewish people often feel as if they come up short, and tend to lack self-esteem. They strive continually to feel good about themselves, sometimes by doing socially responsible things. I call it the social-worker syndrome. Some of those who do the most for humanity have the lowest quantity of self-esteem. I've seen it over and over.

You can offer your neighbor unconditional acceptance, the kind of acceptance God offers us in the Messiah. You can contribute to fulfilling your Jewish friend's need for self-esteem. This will lead him or her to the last level Maslow described, self-actualization.

Self-actualization, as I said earlier, is considered the ability to achieve one's highest potential. I am not supportive of what is called "the human potential movement" or any of the "me-oriented" schools of psychology that leave God out of the picture. Maslow's model, however, enables us to discuss needs. I do think that the fulfillment of humankind's highest potential is found only through reconciliation with God through Yeshua. Once a person accepts

God's offer of eternal and abundant life, then God can guide him to be more like the Messiah, to be caring, giving, a true contributor to society—not based on a need for self-esteem, but based on a desire to serve others.

Many Jewish people have been involved in the human potential movement, more recently known as "secular humanism." Maslow, himself a Jew, was at the forefront of the movement. The founder of modern psychology, Sigmund Freud, also was Jewish. As I mentioned earlier, there has been a disproportionate number of Jews involved in self-help philosophies and "pseudo-spiritual" cults. Jews, who in many ways feel they have successfully completed their first four levels, are now seeking self-actualization.

I have seen many of these men and women leave their respective cults and become believers in the Messiah once they discovered that true self-actualization can come only when we look into the face of God, not repeat a *mantra* or fondle a crystal as so many do today. I am encouraged that so many of my fellow Jewish people are on a spiritual search. And I am thankful that *you* will be there when they realize they have been heading down the wrong road.

Yeshua was going to deal with the spiritual need of the woman at the well, but first He had to bring her face-to-face with this need. He began with the mention of living water, water that would last forever. She longed for this water so that she would never have to come and draw water again.

Please pray that you can understand the needs of your Jewish neighbor and communicate creatively in such a way that he or she will want to hear more.

## Establish Credibility

We spoke earlier about credibility, that extra something that makes one person more believable than another. You can develop a more credible testimony with every encounter. The way you relate to your family says something about how your faith operates. Your business dealings reveal further the reliability of that faith. Your works testify to the worth of your belief. Each of these adds to or detracts from your credibility quotient.

In John 4:16–19, Yeshua uses His supernatural powers to establish a supernatural credibility. We, too, can exhibit unusual insight when witnessing to our Jewish friends. Therefore, it will be worth looking at how Yeshua established His credibility. Remember, up until this point He was just a tired, hungry, thirsty Jew who was violating Jewish tradition!

> He said to her, "Go, call your husband, and come here." The woman answered and said, "I have no husband." Jesus said to her, "You have well said, 'I have no husband'; for you have had five husbands; and the one whom you now have is not your husband; this you have said truly." The woman said to Him, "Sir, I perceive that You are a prophet. . . ."

He knew her heart. He knew her darkest secrets. He knew she was a sinner, yet He did not condemn her. Somehow, this Jew she had never met before knew everything about her. *How amazing!* she must have thought. Perhaps this man was some sort of prophet. Perhaps she could ask him some religious questions. And this is exactly what she did as we shall see.

Jewish people, like all people, yearn to know about the spiritual world. They watch shows about the occult, mysticism, and the supernatural and long to know what it's all about. But whom can they ask? You would hope they would turn automatically to their rabbis. But rabbis teach more about morality and *mitzvot* than about the spiritual realm and the supernatural.

It's the rare rabbi who emphasizes teachings about angels, demons, heaven, hell, the Messiah, or the resurrection. This is not the content of your average Sabbath morning sermon. You might hear a talk on an abstract force we historically call God. You might be treated to a treatise on how to be a good parent. You might listen to a discussion of traditions or holiday celebrations. Oh, sure, there are readings from the Tenakh and often the readings serve as a jumping-off point for the sermon. But too often what is missing is a sense of reality concerning Bible events. Somehow, I'm sad to say, many of my people have lost their sense of the supernatural, relegating God to the status of rabbinical tradition.

Often the miracles of the Bible are described as mere natural events that a superstitious and backward people attributed to what they called God. It would not be surprising to hear discussion of "the myths of the Bible." The sense of awe has vanished from the worship of the majority of Jewish people.

For the most part, then, Jews would not go to their rabbis to discuss issues of the supernatural. But, oddly enough, they might come to you if they are convinced that you truly believe in the supernatural. You may have the opportunity to explain things to your Jewish neighbor that he or she might not find answers to anywhere else—information concerning the Bible or God or the afterlife.

As I shared before, when I met the Rigneys, who led me to the Lord, I was very thirsty to talk about spiritual things. One rabbi I spoke to was controlled by the Talmud and wouldn't discuss certain forbidden subjects. The other rabbi didn't even believe in God. My spiritual thirst demanded answers. The Rigneys were trustworthy and knowledgeable about the Bible as well as the Jewish people; I had plenty to ask them. They had answers.

Your Jewish friend may be thirsting for information about spiritual things. He or she may have wrestled with questions for decades. If you display evidence of credibility, your neighbor might ask *you.*

## Open Up the Scriptures

The woman at the well sensed Yeshua's credibility. He knew all about her and still He talked to her. He accepted her, a major-league sinner. He was trustworthy and expert, two of the three factors that make a person credible. Here was an opportunity to ask questions that may have been bothering her for years:

> "Our fathers worshiped in this mountain [Gerizim]; and you people say that in Jerusalem is the place where men ought to worship."
>
> JOHN 4:20

Even though it sounded like a statement, this lady was asking an implied question. Yeshua heard it, and answered her:

Jesus said to her, "Woman, believe Me, an hour is coming when neither in this mountain, nor in Jerusalem, shall you worship the Father. You worship that which you do not know; we worship that which we know, for salvation is from the Jews. But an hour is coming, and now is, when the true worshipers shall worship the Father in spirit and truth; for such people the Father seeks to be His worshipers. God is spirit, and those who worship Him must worship in spirit and truth."

JOHN 4:21–24

Recognizing Yeshua's credibility, she asked the question about worship—Gerizim or Jerusalem? Yeshua used this opportunity to discuss scriptural subjects. She asked about the place of worship; He answered about salvation, about the nature of God, and about how to worship Him.

The hour of salvation was upon her, He explained. Salvation was to come through the Jews. Furthermore, God had a way He wanted people to worship Him that did not merely involve location—God wanted to be worshiped in spirit and truth.

Keep in mind that it took only a few short minutes for this woman to feel comfortable and trusting enough to talk about these controversial issues. Yeshua was drawing her into the truth. Once He got to the spiritual subjects of salvation and worship, the "close" was not far away.

## Introduce Salvation

Suppose that when this lady with her pitcher of water had approached the well, Yeshua had stood up and said, "Hi, I'm the Messiah. Got a drink?" In modern-day vernacular she might have responded, "Sure, buddy, and I'm the Queen of England." He was tired, hungry, sweaty, dressed in the clothes of a working man, not the royal robes of a king. Not exactly the image of the Messiah! The woman might well have walked away from this "nut." At least she might have avoided further conversation with Him. But Yeshua didn't do this. His approach was slowly revealing; He moved carefully, following through, step by step, until *she* asked *Him* if He might indeed be the Messiah.

The woman said to Him, "I know that Messiah is coming (He who is called Christ); when that One comes, He will declare all things to us." Jesus said to her, "I who speak to you am He."

JOHN 4:25–26

I can't help thinking that she had some hint that He was the Messiah. I hear a question mark at the end of her statement. She was ready. It was time. She believed. She left her water pot and broadcast the news all over town. "This man told me everything about my life. Can He be the Messiah?" How many people believed as a result of hearing her testimony is hard to say. But surely many did. Yeshua caught a lot of fish that day. There's no reason we can't as well.

Yeshua was *willing* to witness. He could have avoided the interaction. He got her *interest*. He did something unusual. He was *timely* in His use of the "living water" image. He spoke to her *need* even though she misinterpreted it. He demonstrated His *expertise* by knowing what she was really like inside. He got into a *scriptural* discussion when she was ready. And, finally, He introduced Himself as the *Savior* when she asked.

A true preacher at heart, I've created an acronym to help you remember these principles. **WITNESS:**

Willingness,
Interest
Timeliness,
Need,
Expertness,
Scripture,
Salvation

The Master Fisherman promised that He would make His disciples fishers of men. May these seven steps help you as you fish—for sheep! For the lost sheep of the house of Israel.

If I can be of any help to you as you set about to share the Messiah, helping you locate your nearest Messianic congregation, supplying you with literature, or answering any questions you might have, contact me at Lederer Messianic Ministries, 6204 Park Heights Ave., Baltimore, MD 21215, (301) 358–6471.

God bless you as you fulfill your Great Commission—and good fishing!

# Epilogue

A few last words of personal testimony. . . .

It was April 15, 1972, an inauspicious day in the minds of most Americans. I was out sailing on the Chesapeake Bay.

We were moving along beneath the Bay Bridge. I looked up to watch some of the construction, marveling at the new span being added to the old bridge. Suddenly the serenity was shattered as a piece of steel tumbled from the bridge, crashing down onto our boat. It landed with an ear-splitting crack, so close to me that it broke my watch crystal. Fortunately, it did not break through the bottom of the boat.

The others I was with raced over to where I stood, their voices high-pitched, full of panic and disbelief. Yet only one thought reached through to my numbed consciousness: Would God bring about something like this to make His point? Scripture teaches that Jews seek for a sign. But this? Or was Satan trying to kill me before I applied what I had heard about salvation in the Messiah?

I found that I was strangely calm about the fact that I had almost been crushed by the piece of falling steel. What made me shake, though, was the enormity of the spiritual decision that lay before me. Although I had studied Isaiah 53, although I had calculated the time of the coming of Messiah in Daniel 9, although I had understood how a Jew could believe in Yeshua, I was still reluctant to yield my life to the Lord.

That night I attended a Passover Seder, the service that recounts the freeing of the Jewish people from slavery in Egypt thousands of years ago. It was a Messianic service led by Dan Rigney. It was held in Baltimore at a place called The Lederer Foundation, the organization for which I now serve as director. I listened as the elements of Passover were described with their full Messianic meaning. I knew I now believed.

That night, in the quietness of my home, I prayed to the God of Abraham, Isaac, and Jacob that Yeshua, His Messiah, would be my Savior.

It was later that I discovered how many people had been praying for me in Baltimore, Washington, and all across the country! From time to time I still meet people who were praying for me back in 1972. One of those people who was praying was a nice Jewish girl originally from the Bronx named Steffi. She and I met a few months after I received Yeshua. We were married two years later and God blessed us with two lovely daughters.

You want your Jewish friend to meet the Messiah. Start to pray; ask others to do the same. We are engaged in spiritual warfare; our most powerful weapon is heartfelt prayer.

So have your neighbor bring the bagels. You bring the Gospel. And I fervently believe that God will bring many new children into His everlasting Kingdom.

# Glossary of Jewish Terms

DEFINITIONS: These are Hebrew and Yiddish words that might be used by Jewish people. (Yiddish is a language spoken by Eastern European Jews that looks a little like Hebrew and sounds somewhat like Hebrew and German. It is spoken by many European and American Jews.) If you understand them, it will help in your contacts with Jewish people.

## Greetings and Good Wishes

| | |
|---|---|
| *Shalom* | peace (used as "hello" or "goodbye") |
| *Shalom Alechem* | peace be unto you |
| *Alechem Shalom* | unto you be peace (a response to the above) |
| *Mazel Tov* | good luck (congratulations). |
| *L'Chayim* | to life! (a toast or salute) |
| *L'Shanah Tovah* | to a good year! (New Year's greeting) |
| *L'Hit Ra'ote* | until we meet again |
| *Chag Samayach* | happy holiday (especially Hanukkah) |
| *Gut Yom Tov* | good holiday |

## Jewish Holidays

| | |
|---|---|
| *Rosh Hashanah* | New Year, celebrated in September or October (Lev. 23:24, 25) |
| *Yom Kippur* | Day of Atonement, observed with fasting and prayer for forgiveness (Lev. 23:26–32) |
| *Kol Nidre* | "All Vows," chanted on the eve of Yom Kippur |
| *Sukkot* | Feast of Tabernacles, celebrated in "booths" (Lev. 23:33–36) |
| *Sukkah* | booth used during *Sukkot* for meals and/or sleeping |
| *Simchat Torah* | Rejoicing Over the Law, concluding the public, synagogal reading of the Torah each year |
| *Hanukkah* | Festival of Lights, celebrating the rededication of the Temple of the Lord by the Maccabees in 167 B.C.E. |

| | |
|---|---|
| *Purim* | Feast of Esther, celebrating the victory over Haman and all who sought Jewish extinction (Esth. 9:20–32) |
| *Pesach* | Passover, the feast of unleavened bread (Ex. 12:14–20) |
| *Seder* | the Passover service (and dinner) usually conducted on the first and second nights of Pesach |
| *Haggadah* | the ritual for the Pesach service, in Hebrew and English, usually |
| *Matzo* | unleavened bread |
| *Shabbat* | the Sabbath (Friday sunset to Saturday sunset) (Lev. 23:3) |
| *Shavuot* | "seven weeks" (from Pesach): Feast of First Fruits (Lev. 23:15–21) |

## Judaism

| | |
|---|---|
| *Barucha* | "blessings," prayer offered on any occasion that calls for praise |
| *Halakhah* | tradition, practice, rule in Judaism |
| *Hallel* | psalms of praise (root word of *hallelujah*) |
| *Minyan* | quorum needed for a service (ten men thirteen years or older) |
| *Siddur* | prayer book (contains prayers, Scripture, order of service) |
| *Menorah* | candleholder: a seven-branch menorah is used (Ex. 25:31–37) except during Hanukkah when a nine-branch menorah is used to remind Jews that a container of oil found when the Temple was being cleansed and rededicated burned for eight days instead of one day—long enough for more oil to be consecrated, according to Scripture |
| *Synagogue* | "assembly" (the same word equivalent as "church"): the use of this word usually indicates either Orthodox or Conservative Judaism |
| *Temple* | the place of worship of Reform Jews |
| *Shule* | another word for an Orthodox or Chassidic synagogue, from the word *school,* it indicates that the |

| | |
|---|---|
| | chief purpose of the synagogue is for the study of the Law (the Torah) |
| *Yeshivah* | a religious school of higher learning |
| *Talmud Torah* | a community religious school teaching Hebrew, Talmud, the Law (Torah), and sometimes secular subjects as well |
| *Mitzvah* | command (in common usage, a good deed) |
| *Bar Mitzvah* | son of the commandment (a boy who has reached the age of religious maturity, age 13, culminating in a special ceremony) |
| *Bat Mitzvah* | daughter of the commandment (a girl who has reached the age of religious maturity, age 12, culminating in a special ceremony) |
| *Bris* or *Brit Milah* | the convenant of circumcision (Gen. 17:9–14) |
| *Chazzan* | cantor, usually the leader of the service |
| *Shammash* | the caretaker or sexton of the synagogue or temple |
| *Yitzkor* | "may he remember": the memorial to the dead and rededication to the spiritual heritage of the Fathers |
| *Kaddish* | "holy": praise to God recited in memorial to the departed |
| *Yahrzeit* | death anniversary (the tombstone unveiling ceremony is conducted on the first anniversary of death. Each year's observance of the anniversary is made at home, by the lighting of a special candle, and at synagogue) |
| *Shiva* | the seven-day mourning period interrupted only on the Sabbath or major holidays |
| *Mikvah* | "immerse": the ritual bath of purification |
| *Chuppah* | the bridal canopy denoting God's presence in the new home and a reminder of the Temple at Jerusalem, symbolic of God's dwelling place with man |
| *Ketubah* | Jewish marriage contract |
| *Ner Tamid* | a perpetual light signifying God's presence |
| *Ruach Ha Kodesh* | the Holy Spirit. |

| | |
|---|---|
| *Mezuzah* | a parchment scroll usually in a metal container attached to the doorpost on the right side of the entrance to a house or room (Deut. 6:9), containing the Sh'ma (Deut. 6:4–11) and the *Vehoyo Shamon* (Deut. 11:13–21); also worn as jewelry |
| *Kiddush* | benediction over the "fruit of the vine" (wine) in the ceremony of sanctification of *Shabbat* and holidays |
| *Yarmulka* | a skullcap used to cover men's heads especially during worship in the synagogue or home (or, *kippa* —"covering") |
| *Tallit* | prayer shawl worn by men during worship in the synagogue or at home |
| *Tzitzit* | the fringes attached to the four corners of the *tallit* (Num. 15:38–40) |
| *Tefillin* | leather boxes attached to leather thongs wound around the head and arm, used by very religious Jews during prayer. The box contains portions of the Torah (Deut. 6:8); also called *"phylacteries"* |
| *The Sh'ma* | Jewish affirmation of faith (Deut. 6:4) recited morning and evening by religious Jews and during all worship services |
| *Kashrut* | "kosher": clean, acceptable food in accordance with Jewish law, especially excluding pork and shellfish (Deut. 14:3–21) |
| *Trefe* | unclean, forbidden food |
| *Torah* | the five books of Moses, the "Law," also known as the *Chumash* |
| *Nevi'im* | the prophets (books of prophecy) |
| *Ketuvim* | the writings (including history and poetry) |
| *Megillot* | "scrolls": part of the *Ketuvim,* including the books of Esther (known as *The Megillah*), Lamentations, Song of Solomon, Ruth, and Ecclesiastes |
| *Tenakh* | Torah, *Nevi'im, Ketuvim* (TeNaK): the Old Testament |

| | |
|---|---|
| *Haftorah* | the section of the prophets read immediately after the reading of the Torah in the services on *Shabbat* and on most holidays |
| *Talmud* | "study"; the oral traditions, discussions, and instructions in 37 volumes (English) of the great rabbis of Judaïsm (100 B.C.E. to 200 C.E.). Commentary on the Tenakh, called "the oral tradition" |
| *Shulchan Aruch* | the codified laws of rabbinical Judaism |
| *Kabbalah* | Jewish mysticism |
| *Tzaddik* | "righteous one": usually applied to a spiritual leader, one who is learned and pious |

## Miscellaneous

| | |
|---|---|
| *Magen David* | shield of David: a six-pointed star commonly worn by Jews and used as a symbol of the Jewish people |
| *Ha Tikvah* | "The Hope": Israel's national anthem |
| *Eretz Yisrael* | the land of Israel |
| *Adonai* | "Lord": no Hebrew word for "God" is used by Jews; *Ha Shem*, "the Name," is used instead; *God* is too holy so His name is not to be pronounced |
| *Mashiach* | Messiah, "Anointed One" |
| *Goy* | nation, Gentile (plural - *goyim*) |
| *Hassid* | "pious one": follower of *Hassidism* |
| *Meshumad* | an apostate Jew, especially one who "converts" to "Christianity" |
| *Sephardi* | a Jewish person from Eastern, Oriental or Southern Mediterranean origins (Turkey, Spain, Egypt, etc.) |
| *Ashkenazi* | a Jew from Central or Western European origin (Poland, Russia, Germany, France, etc.) |
| *Zion* | Israel |
| *Zionist* | one who supports the idea of a Jewish state, namely, Israel |
| *Aliyah* | "going up": making a first visit to *Eretz Yisrael*, a pilgrimage |
| *B'nai B'rith* | "sons of the covenant": a Jewish fraternal organization founded in 1843 |